THE POCKET GUIDE TO
BIRDS OF WESTERN NORTH AMERICA

THE POCKET GUIDE TO BIRDS OF WESTERN NORTH AMERICA

FRANK SHAW

DRAGON'S WORLD

Dragon's World Ltd
Limpsfield
Surrey RH8 0DY
Great Britain

First published by Dragon's World 1990

Illustrations by Norman Arlott, Trevor Boyer, Malcolm Ellis, Robert Morton, Maurice Pledger, Christopher Rose and David Thelwell of Bernard Thornton Artists, London.

British Library Cataloguing in Publication Data

Shaw, Frank
The pocket guide to birds of western north America.
1. Western North America. Birds
I. Title
598.297

ISBN 1-85028-093-2

Editor: Michael Downey
Designer: Peter Ward
Editorial Director: Pippa Rubinstein

Typeset by Action Typesetting Ltd, Gloucester, England
Printed in Singapore

Contents

Introduction 6

Loons and Grebes 9
Petrels and Shearwaters 14
Pelicans, Gannets and Cormorants 16
Swans, Geese and Ducks 19
Birds of Prey 37
Grouse 48
Herons and Rails 57
Shorebirds 66
Gulls, Terns, Auks 87
Pigeons and Cuckoos 104
Owls 108
Nightjars, Swifts and Hummingbirds 116
Woodpeckers and Flickers 124
Flycatchers 132
Larks and Swallows 141
Crows and Jays 145
Chickadees, Nuthatches, Wrens and Thrashers 150
Thrushes, Pipits and Starlings 166
Vireos and Warblers 176
Blackbirds and Orioles 192
Finches and Grosbeaks 201
Sparrows 213

Index 227

Introduction

The field guide is as essential a tool to the birder as are his or her binoculars. Without some means of naming birds, all observations become both unstructured and pointless. By definition, a field guide is designed to be of use 'in the field', out there where the birds are, rather than at home in the bookshelf. It must, therefore, be portable rather than tome-like, it should be durable and it should be precise. Sadly, these qualities pose tricky problems for publishers, artists and authors who want their books to meet all of these criteria, but still manage to hold all the detail that is required to fulfil the field guide's primary aim – to accurately identify every bird likely to be encountered.

Some birds, such as the Robin, are familiar and easily identified. Such birds need little in the way of either illustration or text. Many of the buteos are, however, very similar as well as varying enormously in plumage within the species. These birds require more illustration and more text. In fact, one could write a book on the identification of North American birds of prey alone. The problem here is that portability soon disappears and a field guide turns into a manual.

Similarly, it is a temptation to include every bird that has ever appeared in a particular region, state, country or life zone. Thus the birds of North America, for example, would include every European and Asiatic waif that had ever struggled to our shores, even though the chances of anyone seeing them are extremely remote. Every field guide is thus a compromise between completeness and portability.

This book covers all the birds that one is likely to see in the western part of North America, rather than every bird of the whole continent. In this way it maintains the criteria of portability. There is a companion volume that covers eastern birds, but each volume is self-sufficient and there is thus a degree of overlap. By covering only half the continent we have not only kept each guide within a reasonable size, but also managed to give more space to each of the birds. This means that the text can vary in length according to the difficulty of identification rather than be restricted to a few lines.

We have also eliminated some birds that have occurred in western North America, but which are either rare vagrants (mainly from Asia to islands in the Bering Straits), or which are restricted to marginal areas of the region. For example, there are several typically Mexican birds which cross over south-eastern borders, but they are never found anywhere else on the continent. Those who wish to see them will know exactly what they are looking for and where to find them.

When deciding where to draw the boundary between west and east it was relatively easy to see that the foothills of the Rockies formed a natural division. We have followed a line from the Yukon border on the Beaufort Sea in the Canadian arctic southwards to north-eastern Saskatchewan. Entering the United States we crossed eastern Montana, Wyoming and Colorado before clipping western Oklahoma and entering northern Texas. The line ends half way along the Texas-Mexico border on the Rio Grande. Within this vast and rich area no less than 436 birds can be regarded as regular. These are the birds covered in this guide.

The birds are arranged in the scientific, or systematic, order adopted by all serious books and publications. Beginners often have difficulty in finding their way around this arrangement and argue that it would be better to arrange birds alphabetically, or according to size, or even habitat. While there is some force to this argument it is relatively easy to learn the basic structure of the systematic order by using it frequently. After a while it becomes second nature to look for herons near the front, gulls in the middle and sparrows at the end. This systematic approach has, however, one overwhelming advantage – it shows the relationships between birds and groups similar species together. Thus if one sees a heron it is a simple matter to flick through the pages and find all the herons placed together.

Each bird has a scientific, as well as an English, name. The names used here follow the American Ornithologists' Union Check List of 1983, though more recent changes have been incorporated and we have followed the general movement towards a standardised list of English names for all the birds in the world. Thus we use the name American Robin rather than plain Robin; Common Redpoll rather than Redpoll. Eventually there will be a universally accepted list of English names. We hope that, in the meantime, the use of these 'qualifying' adjectives will become more widely used.

Identifying birds is partly an art and partly a science, the key is knowledge. Confronted by an unknown bird, the secret of identification is knowing what to look for. This knowledge can be acquired from books, or by actively pursuing birds in the field. As with so many other skills, a combination of the two is probably the best method. Learning that gulls are often identified by their wing tips; that shorebirds require close attention to be paid to their rump patterns; that flycatchers can be divided by the presence or absence of wingbars and eye rings and so on, can be learned without ever setting sight on a bird. But there is no substitute for practice with the actual bird before one's binoculars.

Some birds are easily identified and quickly become familiar. Others, often because they are seen less frequently, remain a problem. Carrying a field guide with one at all times is a vital element in the learning process. It enables every bird seen to be correctly named, but it also acts as a source of background knowledge when checking an unknown locality, or exploring a new habitat. Always remember that not all birds are as widely distributed as the Robin, nor are they so catholic in their choice of habitat as the Starling. Spotting a Kirtland's Warbler in a Texas backyard is about as likely as seeing an Acorn Woodpecker in Central Park, New York. Birds are creatures of habit and knowing as much as possible about their habits can prevent foolish misidentifications.

The field guide also acts as a crammer, a means by which one can learn in advance what one is looking for in particular birds. Using a field guide as bed-time reading every night is a sure method of getting to know unfamiliar birds, though it may not be conducive to sleep. Puzzling through the warblers and flycatchers can exercise the best of minds, but there is no better method of learning their field marks. Similarly, bus, train and plane journeys all offer opportunities to 'mug-up' particular bird groups so that, confronted by a bird, one knows what to look for.

Just where bird identification moves from the field of science (knowledge) to art (feeling) is difficult to say. Perhaps it varies with individuals. Somewhere along the line, however, one starts to name birds at a glance, often without seeing a single field mark. Such skill is the result of a combination of knowledge and experience. Suddenly an Accipiter becomes an Accipter rather than a confusing bird of prey on the pages of the field guide. A crane is a crane, not a heron; a warbler a warbler, not a sparrow; a jaeger a jaeger, not an immature gull. Somehow one has acquired a sense of a bird's character, a combination of shape, structure and behavior that is unique to a particular bird that enables it to be identified instantly and at great distance. This is birding as an art and, therefore, difficult to define or explain. To the beginner it seems impossible to acquire such skill, but never despair – the rule is learn and practice, learn and practice, and practice and practice.

Top birders are obsessed. But even if you have no ambitions to be a top birder and just do not seem able to catch the obsession, don't worry. Birding is a lovely way of spending time. Not everyone can be a Gary Player or a Jack Nicklaus, but that does not stop millions of Americans beating a ball around a golf course every weekend. Enjoy your birding, even if you never manage an identification 'par round'.

All birds depicted are adult males in summer plumage with the exception of the three phalaropes, which are female.

Common Loon

Gavia immer 27–37in/68–81cm

Identification A large, duck-like bird that dives easily. In summer, black head and boldly checkered back separate from all divers except Yellow-billed Loon which has pale ivory bill. In winter, back is barred gray and large, pointed, black bill is held horizontally. White extends above eye. *See* Yellow-billed Loon.
Voice Wild wailing cries in summer.
Habitat Lakes in summer; coasts in winter.
Range Breeds throughout Canada to US borders.
Movements Winters west and east coasts of Canada and US, including Gulf Coast.

Yellow-billed Loon

Gavia adamsii 33–39in/84–99cm

Identification Very similar to Common Loon, but separated at all times by large, pale bill with sharply, upwards-angled lower mandible. This creates impression of uptilted bill. Plumage pattern closely resembles Common Loon in both summer and winter.
Voice Wailing cries in summer.
Habitat Tundra lakes in summer; coasts in winter.
Range Breeds in western Canadian arctic.
Movements Migrates through Alaska to winter on west coast of Canada. Rare southwards.

Arctic Loon

Gavia arctica 23–27in/58–68cm

Identification In summer, distinguished by gray crown, black throat, checkered back and boldly striped neck. In winter is the darkest of all the loons, with dark crown extending to below the eye. At this time most likely to be confused with the Common Loon, but white patch on rear flank can be helpful.
Voice Loud wailings in summer.
Habitat Large lakes in summer; coasts in winter.
Range Breeds throughout Alaska, eastwards through Canadian arctic, south of tree line.
Movements Winters west coast of Canada and US.

Red-throated Loon

Gavia stellata 21–23in/53–58cm

Identification Smallest of the loons. In summer, has gray head with rusty throat and striped nape and hind neck. At this season, is only loon that lacks checker-board back. In winter is grayer above than other loons. Thin bill always held uptilted.
Voice Wailing and cackling in summer.
Habitat Breeds on small lakes moving to sea or larger lakes to feed; winters along coasts.
Range Breeds coastal and tundra Canada.
Movements Moves southwards to winter on east and west coasts and along southern shores of Great Lakes.

Western Grebe

Aechmophorus occidentalis 22–29in/56–74cm

Identification Largest of grebes, with exceptionally long neck and bill. Upper parts dark gray, extending up hind neck to form a black cap that is curiously 'bumped' at rear. White 'face' and foreneck prominent at a distance. In flight, shows white bar across wing. Elaborate dancing display.

Voice *Kr-r-rick,* especially in summer.
Habitat Lakes in summer; coasts in winter.
Range Breeds on lakes of the west as far as the prairie lakes.
Movements Winters along west coast of British Columbia and the US as far as Mexico.

Red-necked Grebe

Podiceps grisegena

15½–18in/40–46cm

Identification Medium-sized grebe. In summer, black cap, silvery 'face' and rust-red neck are distinctive. In winter, a black cap, whitish 'face' and dusky foreneck are best identification features. Size and substantial bill should separate from smaller grebes at all times.
Voice Wailing and loud *keck-keck* when breeding.
Habitat Lakes with plentiful emergent vegetation; mainly coastal in winter.
Range Breeds from Alaska to the Great Lakes in Canada and to the US border country.
Movements Some birds migrate across the eastern US to winter along the Atlantic coasts; others winter along Pacific coasts as far south as California.

Horned Grebe

Podiceps auritus 12–14in/31–36cm

Identification A colorful grebe in summer with black head and golden 'horns' extending as a crest. Foreneck and underparts are rust-red. In winter, dark above and white below with distinctive capped appearance and white foreneck. Bill thickish and pointed. *See* Eared Grebe.
Voice Various squealing notes.
Habitat Marshy lakes and ponds in summer; coastal in winter.
Range Breeds over most of western Canada, except extreme north.
Movements Migrates across northern US to winter on Atlantic coasts, along Central Flyway to Gulf Coast and along Pacific coast as far as California.

Eared Grebe

Podiceps nigricollis

11–13in/28–33cm

Identification Only a trifle smaller than Horned Grebe. In summer, head and neck black, with a gold fan on sides of 'face'. Breast black, underparts and flanks rusty. In winter, is dark above and white below. Cap darkish with paler hind crown, foreneck dusky not white as Horned Grebe. Bill, thin and uptilted at all times.
Voice Quiet *poo-cep* plus various raucous notes.
Habitat Marshes and ponds in summer; winters on coasts and large lakes.
Range Breeds in prairie zone of western Canada southwards over much of western US.
Movements Winters along Pacific coast, but many move southwards into Mexico.

Pied-billed Grebe

Podilymbus podiceps 12–15in/30–38cm

Identification A thick-set, chunky grebe with large conical bill. Upperparts brown, with boldly barred brown and buff flanks and square-cut white rear end. In summer, there is a bold black patch on the throat and the heavy, pale bill has a vertical black bar near the tip. In winter, throat and bill are both whitish. Pale eye-ring at all times.
Voice Various yelping calls.
Habitat Shallow ponds with vegetation in summer; plus larger waters in winter.
Range Breeds throughout US and southern Canada.
Movements Leaves northern and central parts of range in winter.

Least Grebe

Tachybaptus dominicus 8–10in/20–25cm

Identification Tiny grebe with dusky gray head, neck and upperparts in summer, but barred buffy on flanks. Bold yellow eye and tiny dark bill are best field marks. In winter, upperparts are less dusky and throat is white.
Voice Distinctive clanging note.
Habitat Overgrown ponds.
Range Breeds southern Texas; but distinctly local.
Movements Resident.

Northern Fulmar

Fulmaris glacialis

17–19½in/44–50cm

Identification A large, gull-like seabird that flies, shearwater-like, on stiff wings. Pale gray above, white below with a short, stubby yellow bill. At all times the thick neck is a good feature.
Voice Harsh cackling at breeding sites.
Habitat Breeds on remote northern cliffs, otherwise at sea, often well out of sight of land.
Range Breeds among Canadian archipelago as far south as Newfoundland and on islands of southern Alaska.
Movements Winters in Pacific and northern Atlantic, may be abundant around fishing vessels.

Manx Shearwater

Puffinus puffinus 12–15in/30–38cm

Identification A typical shearwater that careers over the sea showing alternately black upperparts and white underparts. Could be confused with Audubon's Shearwater, but is larger, longer-winged and less fluttering in flight.
Voice Silent at sea.
Habitat Oceans.
Range Regular offshore along Californian coast, rare off coast of eastern Canada.
Movements Breeds in Europe and on islands off the coast of Baja California in Mexico. Mostly in North America in fall.

Sooty Shearwater

Puffinus griseus 15–17in/39–44cm

Identification A dusky, medium-sized shearwater. Upperparts are uniformly dusky-brown; underparts similar, but with a distinctive pale center to the underwing. Though a typical shearwater, the long wings are held slightly more angled than other species and flight is more flapping.
Voice Silent at sea.
Habitat Oceans.
Range Breeds only in Southern Hemisphere. Fall visitor to east coast (scarce) and west coast (common).
Movements Regular loop migration into both Pacific and Atlantic Oceans when not breeding.

Leach's Storm-Petrel

Oceanodroma leucorhoa 7½–8½in/19–22cm

Identification Small, black seabird with forked tail and bold white rump. In flight, shows gray coverts extending across the upper wing. In southern California white rump is absent. Feet do not extend beyond tail, seldom follows ships. Flight consists of glides and wing flapping.
Voice Various screeches and crooning at breeding colonies.
Habitat Breeds on remote islands; winters at sea.
Range Breeds along western coasts and in the north-east from Labrador to Maine.
Movements Disperses at sea.

Brown Pelican

Pelecanus occidentalis 45–54in/114–137cm

Identification Unmistakable, being the only pelican that dives for its food. In summer, adult is silvery-brown with large, dark-brown bill and pouch, creamy neck and chestnut hind-neck and foreneck. In winter the chestnut is lost. Juvenile is brown and whitish, with dark upperparts. In flight, dark body contrasts with pale head. Usually gregarious.
Voice Nestlings produce wide variety of calls; adults silent.
Habitat Sea coasts and lagoons.
Range Breeds along both Pacific and Atlantic coasts and along Gulf Coast.
Movements Largely resident.

American White Pelican

Pelecanus erythrorhynchos 55–70in/140–178cm

Identification Unmistakable huge, white bird with large orange-pink bill and pouch. Adult is all white save for the bill; and for black flight feathers that are particularly apparent in the air. Juvenile has brown crown and bill, but dirty white body. Flies in formation on broad wings.
Voice Usually silent.
Habitat Marshes and lagoons.
Range Breeds in central west Canada southwards to California and Texas.
Movements Winters along coasts and inland in California and Gulf Coast.

Northern Gannet

Sula bassana 34–38in/86–96cm

Identification Large black and white seabird that gathers at enormous colonies in favored localities. Large, cigar-shaped body with pointed head and tail. Long, stiffish wings with boldly black tips. Flies with series of flaps and long glides, dives from air into sea. Juveniles dark brown, becoming whiter over several years.
Voice Grunts and cackles at colonies.
Habitat Remote islands and stacks; winters at sea.
Range Breeds on islands off Newfoundland, Nova Scotia and in Gulf of St Lawrence.
Movements Disperses over seas as far south as Florida and adjacent Gulf Coast in winter.

Brandt's Cormorant

Phalacrocorax penicillatus

33–35in/84–89cm

Identification Uniformally black cormorant marked by difficult-to-see blue throat patch bordered by a dull creamy patch that is a much better field mark. Shiny, iridescent plumage, lacks a crest.
Voice Croaks and grunts while breeding.
Habitat Coastal, breeds on offshore rocks.
Range Breeds from southern British Columbia to Mexico and confined to Pacific.
Movements Local dispersal only.

Double-crested Cormorant

Phalacrocorax auritus

30½–36in/77–91cm

Identification All-dark cormorant with golden sheen on wings like Great Cormorant. The most common and widespread member of the family. Orange-red 'face' is almost the only distinguishing feature; the double crests are virtually impossible to see in the field. Juveniles are buffy below, brown above and show orange-red on face.
Voice Grunts while breeding.
Habitat Lakes, rivers and coastal waters.
Range Breeds throughout most of US and temperate Canada, though absent from hilly and mountain areas.
Movements Winters along most coasts and inland along southern river systems.

Pelagic Cormorant

Phalacrocorax pelagicus

25–30in/64–76cm

Identification A small, all-black cormorant with thin bill and neck. A white flank patch develops during the breeding season and the 'face' is bright red at all times. A double crest marks the crown, but is visible only at close range. Juvenile is brown with only structure to aid identification.
Voice Grunts at breeding colony.
Habitat Coasts and offshore waters.
Range Breeds from Bering Straits to central California.
Movements Local dispersal along Pacific Coast.

Whistling Swan

Cygnus columbianus

47–58in/119–147cm

Identification Most common and widespread of the swans. Adult is white with long straight neck and black bill. There is usually a small spot of yellow in front of the eye. Juvenile is gray-brown with dull, pinkish bill.
Voice Goose-like whistled call.
Habitat Marshy tundra ponds in summer; coastal marshes and inland floods in winter.
Range Breeds on western Canadian tundra.
Movements Migrates southwards to winter at traditional sites on Atlantic and Pacific coasts and at a few inland sites in the west.

Trumpeter Swan

Cygnus buccinator 59–71in/150–180cm

Identification Very large swan with proportionately longer neck than Whistling Swan. Neck mostly held straight; bill black with narrow orange margin to lower mandible. Juvenile is gray-brown with pink bill marked by extensive black areas.
Voice Loud trumpeting calls.
Habitat Wild and remote marshes.

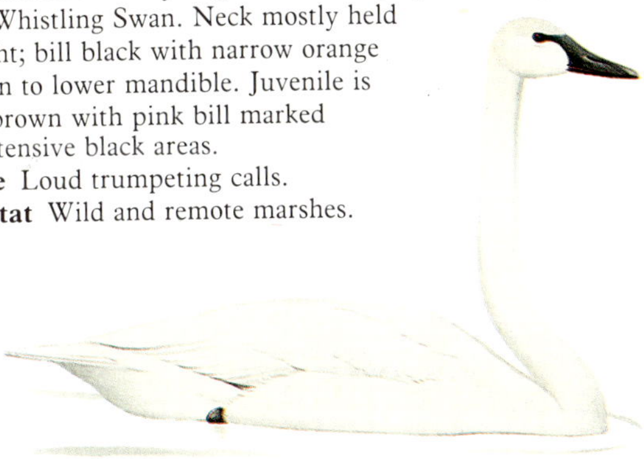

Range Once in danger of extinction but has now increased in two native areas on Alaska-Canada border and in Montana. A reintroduction programme has re-established former populations in west.
Movements Winters on breeding areas and nearby ice-free areas.

Canada Goose

Branta canadensis 22–36in/56–92cm

Identification Highly variable in size. Brown and buff body, with long black neck and head, with white area on side extending from chin. Abundant, noisy, well-known.
Voice Loud honking, especially in flight.
Habitat Marshes, lakes.

Range Breeds right across Canada extending southwards through the prairies and Rockies. Small race of Alaska-Yukon known as 'Cackling Goose'.
Movements Migrates throughout Canada and US to winter along Pacific and Atlantic coasts and in temperate US.

Brant

Branta bernicla 23–26in/58–66cm

Identification Small, brown and buff goose with black breast, neck and head, broken by white slash on side of neck. Bill small and delicate. Essentially a gregarious, shore-line bird in winter. This bird breeds right around the northern pole in the tundra zone and has developed several well-marked sub-species. In North America the western sub-species is often treated separately as Black Brant. It differs in having a black belly with pale flanks.
Voice A honking *rank-rank*.
Habitat Tundra in summer, shores and adjacent marshes in winter.
Range High Canadian arctic.
Movements Moves southward to winter along Pacific and Atlantic coasts.

White-fronted Goose

Anser albifrons

25½–30in/65–76cm

Identification A small, gray goose that is easily identified. Basically, barred brown and buff above, with buffy underparts marked by bold black smudges. The base of the bill and forehead are white, the bill pink and the legs orange. Juvenile lacks white forehead and black belly smudging. Birds from Greenland have orange bills.

Voice High-pitched honking.

Habitat Breeds on tundra; winters on grasslands near coast.

Range Western Canadian arctic tundra.

Movements Migrates to west coast and through Central Flyway to Gulf Coast.

Snow Goose

Anser caerulescens 25–31in/64–79cm

Identification A small goose that is abundant in major breeding and wintering grounds. Adult is pure white with black wing tips and pink bill and legs. Dark phase birds are found in the eastern part of the breeding range and are known as the Blue Goose. They have white head, but blue-brown body and wings.

Voice Nasal, muffled honking.

Habitat Tundra in summer; winters on marshes.

Range From northern Alaska through Canadian arctic to Baffin Island.

Movements Uses all three flyways to winter on Pacific, Atlantic and Gulf Coasts. Also inland in California and elsewhere.

Ross's Goose

Chen rossii 21–25½in/53–65cm

Identification Very similar to Snow Goose with all-white plumage, black wing tips, pink bill and legs. Much, much smaller and daintier with smaller bill.
Voice Various cackling calls.
Habitat Breeds on tundra; winters on marshes.
Range Breeds in restricted area of Canadian tundra west of Hudson's Bay.
Movements Follows narrow path southwards to winter in Sacramento Valley of California.

Mallard

Anas platyrhynchos 21½–24½in/55–62cm

Identification Widespread and common duck over much of North America. Male has bottle-green head, white neck ring and brown throat. Upperparts are gray, underparts a pale silver with a black rear end. In flight, there is a blue speculum bordered white. Female is mottled in shades of brown with orange bill.

Voice Loud quacking.
Habitat Ponds, lakes, rivers, marshes, estuaries.
Range Breeds through most of boreal and temperate Canada south through the northern US.
Movements Much of the northern part of the breeding range is abandoned as birds move southwards to winter throughout US.

Northern Pintail

Anas acuta 21–27½in/53–70cm

Identification A slim, elegant duck with extended central tail feathers. Male is delicately colored with a chocolate-brown hood extending to the neck and with various shades of gray on the body terminating in a black and white rear end. The central tail feathers form the pin-tail. Female is mottled in shades of gray-brown. Both sexes have delicate blue bills, long necks and pointed tails.
Voice Quacks.
Habitat Marshes, estuaries.
Range Breeds across eastern half of Canada into Alaska and southward into the eastern US.
Movements Winters on coasts and in southern half of US.

Gadwall

Anas strepera

19–21½in/48–54cm

Identification At a distance, male resembles female of other surface-feeding ducks, but a close approach reveals a fine pattern of vermiculated grays. Most obvious feature is black rear end and white speculum. Female similar to female Mallard with orange bill; but white speculum separates when seen. Smaller, more round-headed than Mallard.
Voice Quacks.
Habitat Marshes, lakes, estuaries.
Range Breeds in north-western US to California and south-western Canada.
Movements Migrates through the US to winter on both coasts and southern half of the country.

American Wigeon

Anas americana 17–19½in/44–50cm

Identification Common duck that forms large flocks at favored areas. Male (formerly Baldpate) has creamy-gray head with bold slash of dark green extending from the eye. Underparts are rufous and separated from the brown upperparts by a bold white lateral line. Female is more subdued and lacks green eye slash. Both have small, gray bills. Spends much time grazing. White inner wing only on male in flight.
Voice Soft whistling.
Habitat Coastal and inland marshes and floods.
Range Breeds from Alaska, through western Canada to north-western US.
Movements Migrates through whole of US to winter on all coasts and in southern states.

Northern Shoveler

Anas clypeata 18½–21in/47–53cm

Identification Both sexes have large spatulate bill. Male has green head, chestnut belly and flanks and boldly white breast that is often best feature when resting. Female is like other surface-feeding ducks, but huge bill always apparent. In flight, pale blue inner wing is useful.
Voice Quacking.
Habitat Shallow marshes, ponds, estuaries.
Range Breeds from Alaska, through western Canada to north-western US.
Movements Migrates through US to winter on all coasts and in southern states.

Blue-winged Teal

Anas discors 14–15½in/36–40cm

Identification Small, Teal-like duck, marked in the male by a slate-blue head with bold white crescent before the eye. Heavily spotted brown on buff below. Female like female Teal, but has pale blue inner wing like the male.

Voice Quiet quacking.
Habitat Ponds, marshes.
Range Breeds over western Canada and US, but not in southern states.
Movements Migrates through US to winter in Florida and along the Gulf Coast.

Cinnamon Teal

Anas cyanoptera 14½–17in/37–43cm

Identification Small duck that looks dark at a distance. Male is, in fact, a deep cinnamon-brown on head and underparts. Upperparts are darkly mottled. Female is mottled in shades of brown. In flight, both show a pale blue forewing like a Blue-winged Teal and pale wing linings contrasting with dark body.
Voice Quacking.
Habitat Marshes, ponds.

Range Breeds over much of western US, extending northwards into adjacent Canada.
Movements Moves southward to winter across Mexican border.

Green-winged Teal

Anas crecca 13½–15in/34–38cm

Identification Common and widespread duck, normally found in flocks. Male has chestnut head broken by green slash through eye, bordered by broken yellow line. Breast is spotted and separated from flanks by vertical white wedge. Rear end is black and cream. Female is like other surface feeding ducks, but with green speculum, bordered white, like male. In flight, white border forms a narrow bar across the wing.

Voice Quacking, whistling.
Habitat Marshes, lakes, estuaries.
Range Breeds in western half of the continent, but not in south-western US.
Movements Migrates throughout US to winter on both coasts and in southern and western states.

Wood Duck

Aix sponsa 17–20in/43–51cm

Identification A woodland duck with bold, multi-colored plumage. Male has harlequin patterned head in purple and white with red bill and eye. The upperparts are an iridescent green, but with chestnut and blue in the wing. Female is spotted below with a gray head broken by white markings, particularly around the eye. In flight, the tail is longer than most other duck.

Voice Whistling *woo-eek.*
Habitat Woodland ponds and rivers.
Range Resident in far western US and summer visitor to eastern half of the country northwards into southern Canada.
Movements Eastern birds migrate to winter in Florida and Gulf Coast.

Fulvous Tree-Duck

Dendrocygna bicolor

18–21in/46–53cm

Identification A gregarious, upright-standing duck that, despite its name, only rarely perches in trees. Head, neck and underparts are barred brown and black. The long neck has a bold white slash. The tail is short, the black legs long and trail in flight.
Voice Whistling.
Habitat Marshes, ponds.
Range In US along Mexican border to Texas and Louisiana Gulf Coast.
Movements Summer visitor to North America.

Redhead

Aythya americana

18–22in/46–56cm

Identification A common diving duck. Male has chestnut-red head, black breast and tail and is gray between the two. The head is rounded and the bill gray with a black tip. It resembles the Canvasback, but is darker gray, has a smaller bill and lacks the wedge-shaped head of that bird. Female is similarly shaped, but patterned in gray-browns with pale eye-ring.
Voice Distinct mewing in breeding season.
Habitat Lakes and ponds; estuaries in winter.
Range Breeds among prairies.
Movements Migrates throughout temperate North America to winter on all coasts.

Canvasback

Aythya valisineria 19½–24in/50–61cm

Identification Very similar to Redhead in plumage pattern, though male is paler gray on body and female grayer throughout. Longer neck and elongated wedge-shaped head with all-black bill are best identification features.

Voice Cooing during breeding season.

Habitat Lakes and marshes; winters along sheltered shorelines and bays.

Range Breeds either side of the US-Canada border in the west, extending further northwards than Redhead.

Movements Migrates throughout US to winter along all coastlines.

Ring-necked Duck

Aythya collaris 15½–18in/40–46cm

Identification Male is a boldly black and white duck, with purple sheen on head and green sheen on breast. The back is black and the flanks gray with a white vertical wedge forwards. It bears a strong resemblance to the scaup, but the dark back, white flank wedge and strongly peaked crown distinguish.
Female is mottled in browns, has a white eye-ring and resembles female Redhead; peaked crown of present species separates at reasonable distance. In flight both sexes show gray wing-bar.

Voice Silent.

Habitat Lakes and ponds.

Range Breeds across southern Canada.

Movements Migrates throughout US to winter near all coasts and throughout the southern states.

Greater Scaup

Aythya marila 15–20in/39–51cm

Identification Marine duck outside the breeding season. Male has black head and breast marked bottle-green, whitish flanks, gray back and black tail. Female is brown with bold white area at base of bill. In flight both show white wing-bar extending across whole of wing. *See* Lesser Scaup.

Voice Soft coos in breeding season.

Habitat Tundra lakes; coastal in winter.

Range Breeds Alaska and neighbouring Canada.

Movements Migrates through whole of North America to winter along all coasts.

Lesser Scaup

Aythya affinis 15–18½in/38–47cm

Identification Similar to Greater Scaup. Head and breast of male washed with purple, not green, sheen; flanks grayer. Female closely resembles female Greater Scaup.

In both sexes the white wing-bar is more obvious on the inner wing, rather than extending across the whole wing as in the Greater Scaup. Additionally the black nail on the bill is tiny.

Voice Cooing in summer.

Habitat Marshes; winters lakes, marshes and estuaries. Far less marine than Greater Scaup.

Range Breeds from Alaska across western Canada to the north-western US.

Movements Migrates throughout to winter on all coasts and inland along river systems and ponds of the south.

Common Goldeneye

Bucephala clangula 15½–19in/40–48cm

Identification Neatly proportioned diving duck with distinct wedge-shaped head. Male has bottle-green head with white spot before the eye. Underparts are white, upperparts black, common separated by an area that is white, striped black. Female has dark chocolate-colored head and is mottled gray above and below. Both sexes show white inner wing in flight. *See* Barrow's Goldeneye.
Voice Quacks in summer.
Habitat Marshes and lakes in boreal forest; lakes and coasts in winter.
Range Northern conifer forests across Canada.
Movements Winters on all coasts and inland throughout the US.

Barrow's Goldeneye

Bucephala islandica 16½–20in/42–51cm

Identification Highly localized relative of Goldeneye. Male similar to Common Goldeneye, but has purple, not green, sheen on head and white crescent, not spot, before eye. Black back and white flanks are separated by black area with white spots – not a white area with black lines. The overall effect is to make this a much darker bird than the Common Goldeneye. Female very similar to female Common Goldeneye. Both sexes have steep forehead.
Voice Various notes when breeding.
Habitat Lakes in forest; coastal in winter.
Range Breeds from Alaska through mountains toWyoming and in northern Labrador.
Movements Winters along west coast to California and in east as far as Long Island. More common in west.

Bufflehead

Bucephala albeola 13–15in/33–38cm

Identification Dainty duck of wooded areas. Male is black above, white below, with black head showing broad white slash extending from eye to nape. Female is browner with white oval behind the eye. Large rounded head and small bill.
Voice Whistles and quacks.
Habitat Pools among conifers; winters on lakes, estuaries.
Range Breeds Alaska and western Canada, extending southwards in Rockies.
Movements Winters on all coasts and throughout ice-free US.

Harlequin Duck

Histrionicus histrionicus 16–17½in/41–45cm

Identification Unique 'torrent' duck that is at home among inland rapids and coastal breakers. Male is gray-blue broken by harlequin pattern of bold white slashes; flanks rust-red. Female brownish, with three pale patches on sides of head. Could be confused with female White-winged and Surf Scoter, but has rounded head and tiny bill.
Voice Croaks in summer.
Habitat Torrents in rivers in summer; rocky coasts in winter.
Range From Alaska southwards through Rockies; and in north eastern Canada.
Movements To the nearest coast in the west, moves southward in the east to New England.

Common Eider

Somateria mollissima 21½–24in/55–61cm

Identification Chunky, heavily built seaduck. Male has white head with black cap and dull green nape. The breast and back are whitish, the underparts black. Female is mottled and barred brown. Both sexes have wedge-shaped head with base of bill extending toward the eye.

Voice Loud cooings when breeding.
Habitat Coasts.
Range Breeds on coasts from British Columbia through Alaska and among the Canadian arctic to Newfoundland, Nova Scotia and Maine.
Movements Winters on Pacific coasts as far south as Vancouver and on Atlantic coasts to Carolina.

King Eider

Somateria spectabilis 21–23in/53–59cm

Identification An arctic breeding duck that is rare in temperate waters. Male is white on breast and black on flanks, back and underparts. The head is a unique pattern of white, blue and orange with an orange bill. Female is mottled brown, but with a much smaller bill than female Common Eider and a more rounded head.

Voice Various croaks.
Habitat Coasts.
Range Breeds arctic coasts.
Movements Winters on ice-free coasts as far south as British Columbia in the west and New England in the east.

Oldsquaw

Clangula hyemalis 16–23in/41–58cm

Identification Attractive sea duck with extended central tail feathers, particularly in the male. Unusual in having distinctive summer and winter plumages. Male, black and white in summer; white and black in winter. Female, blotched brown, with smudgy appearance. Rounded head, short bill and overall shape identify in all plumages.
Voice Yodelling calls in summer.
Habitat Tundra pools; winters along coasts.
Range Canadian arctic in breeding season.
Movements Migrates to winter along both east and west coasts and in Great Lakes.

Common Scoter

Melanitta nigra
18–20in/46–51cm

Identification An all-black seaduck. Male, uniformly black with yellow knob at base of bill. Female, dark brown with paler cheek patches. In mixed flocks at a distance at sea, the pale cheeks of the female are often the only detail visible.
Voice Some croaking in summer.
Habitat Tundra lakes; at sea in winter.
Range Breeds in western Alaska, Newfoundland and Labrador.
Movements Migrates along Pacific coast and across Canada to winter on east coast as far south as Carolina.

White-winged Scoter

Melanitta fusca 21–23in/53–59cm

Identification At any distance male closely resembles other scoter, but has white 'eye' and bold white patch in wing. Female brown, with two pale patches on side of head and similar white in wing.
Voice Croaks in summer.
Habitat Lakes; coastal in winter, but some inland on lakes.
Range Breeds from Alaska in broad band through Manitoba and North Dakota.
Movements Migrates to winter on both east and west coasts and in Great Lakes.

Surf Scoter

Melanitta perspicillata 17–21in/43–53cm

Identification Male similar to other scoter at any distance, but close approach reveals patches of white on crown and nape, and boldly-colored orange, red and white bill. Female very closely resembles female White-winged Scoter with similar pale patches on sides of head. Both sexes lack white in wing of that bird.
Voice Croaks in summer.
Habitat Tundra in north-western Canada and in Alaska.
Range Breeds Alaska and north-western and north-eastern Canada.
Movements Winters on all coasts.

Ruddy Duck

Oxyura jamaicensis 14–17in/36–43cm

Identification Small, dumpy duck with curious, weight-forward appearance. Tail often held vertical or hidden in water surface. In summer, male is rich chestnut on body, with white face, black cap and bright blue bill. In winter, the colors are lost and it is clothed in shades of brown. Female mottled brown with distinctive horizontal stripe across 'face'.

Voice Various croaking calls in summer.
Habitat Marshes and ponds.
Range Breeds through prairies north and south of US-Canada border, as well as valleys of Rockies. Small population on east coast.
Movements Migrates throughout US to winter on ice-free waters near all coasts.

Common Merganser

Mergus merganser
22½–27in/57–69cm

Identification Larger and stouter than Red-breasted Merganser with crest that always points downwards. Male is black above, white below with bottle-green head that extends into rounded hind crest. Female similar to female Red-breasted Merganser, but with rounded, down-pointing crest.
Voice Croaks and cackles in summer.
Habitat Freshwater pools and rivers; mostly freshwater in winter.
Range Breeds through conifer belt of Canada extending southwards in the west.
Movements Migrates southwards to winter in northern and central US.

Red-breasted Merganser

Mergus serrator

20–22in/51–56cm

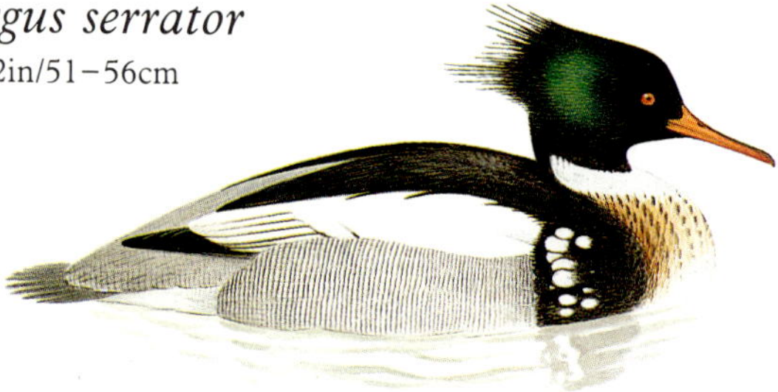

Identification A slim, sawbill duck with ragged crest. Male has bottle green head, white neck, a speckled brown breast, black and white upperparts and gray flanks. The bill is long, thin and red. Female has rufous head and gray body. In all plumages the spiked crest points horizontally to the rear. Male separated from Common Merganser at any distance by speckled, not white breast.
Voice Various purring and croaking calls while breeding.
Habitat Rivers; in winter on creeks and sea.
Range Breeds among tundra from Alaska through northern Canada.
Movements Migrates through much of US to winter on all three coastlines.

Hooded Merganser

Lophodytes cucullatus 15½–19in/40–48cm

Identification Smallest of the sawbills with large, erectile crest. Male has black head with broad, white wedge extending from the eye to the nape in a crest that can be raised or lowered. The breast is white with two narrow bands. Female is like diminutive female Red-breasted Merganser, but crest forms a fan rather than two points. Rather browner above than other female sawbills.

Voice Croaking calls in summer.
Habitat Lakes among woods; winters on lakes near coast.
Range Breeds from coast to coast in a broad area north and south of the US-Canada border.
Movements Winters near all three coastlines.

Turkey Vulture

Cathartes aura 26–32in/66–81cm

Identification Large, dark bird of prey. Plumage basically black with brownish wings. In the air, the flight feathers are paler than the wing linings and the body. Head is bare, wrinkled and red; gray in immatures. Soars and glides on wings held in shallow 'V'. One of the largest birds of prey in America.
Voice Silent.
Habitat Open country, roadsides.
Range Breeds virtually throughout US and across Canadian border in prairies.
Movements Leaves most of northern and central states in winter.

American Black Vulture

Coragyps atratus 23–23½in/58–59cm

Identification All-black bird of prey. The Black Vulture is entirely black, though a silvery sheen shows on the folded wings. The face is bare and black, the bill thin and pointed – not chunky like juvenile Turkey Vulture. In flight the base of the primaries is a bold white. These are gregarious birds that soar on flat wings.
Voice Silent.
Habitat Open country, roadsides and, in the south, shorelines and villages.
Range Resident in southern and eastern states.
Movements May leave northern part of mid-west in winter.

White-tailed Kite

Elanus leucurus

15–17in/38–43cm

Identification Medium-sized bird of prey that hovers like a Kestrel. Adult is gray above with black 'shoulder' patches. Head, underparts and square-cut tail are white. The head is rather large and flat-topped, marked by large eye. In flight the wings are pointed and the bird hovers when hunting.
Voice High pitched yelps.
Habitat Parkland, fields, grasslands with trees.
Range Once rare, now re-established in California, also in southern Texas.
Movements Resident.

Northern Goshawk

Accipiter gentilis

19–23in/48–58cm

Identification Large, dashing accipiter mainly confined to northern forests. The smaller male is gray above and streaked on white below. A bold, white eyebrow creates a fierce expression. Female is larger and browner with heavily barred underparts. These magnificent and powerful birds are agile fliers among trees. They soar easily and show a white powder-puff under the tail in diving display.
Voice High-pitched *kee-kee-kee.*
Habitat Conifer forests, but also deciduous forests to the south.
Range Boreal forests of Canada and conifers in Rockies and north-western US. Extending southwards to deciduous forests recently.
Movements Moves southwards as winter visitor to central US.

Cooper's Hawk

Accipiter cooperii

14–20in/35–51cm

Identification Medium-sized accipiter with rounded wings and long tail. Gray above, barred rusty below with rounded tail showing four or five clear bands. Fast and agile flier that soars with series of fast wing beats interupting still-winged gliding.
Voice High-pitched, repetitive *kee-kee-kee.*
Habitat Deciduous woods, sometimes also conifers.
Range Virtually throughout US and into adjacent Canada, but serious decline and disappearance from many areas of US.
Movements Leaves central and northern parts of range in winter.

Sharp-shinned Hawk

Accipiter striatus 10–14in/25–35cm

Identification Smallest of the accipiters. Gray above and barred rusty below. Rounded wings and long-tailed which is square-ended (Cooper's is rounded) and shows four or five clear dark bands. Agile flier in pursuit of small birds.
Voice High-pitched *ka-ka-ka.*
Habitat Conifer and deciduous forests; virtually any woodland or wooded country in winter.
Range From Alaska through boreal Canada to most of the US except the extreme south.
Movements Leaves northern part of range and most of Canada; winters through most of the US.

Northern Harrier

Circus cyaneus 17–20in/43–51cm

Identification A long-winged, long-tailed bird of prey that flaps and glides low over the ground. Male is gray above and white below, with bold white rump band. Female is mottled brown and buff, but has same white rump.
Voice Sharp *kee-kee-kee* when breeding.
Habitat Marshes, rough grassland.
Range Breeds over much of Alaska, Canada and the northern US.
Movements Winters virtually throughout US, but only locally in southern Canada.

Rough-legged Hawk

Buteo lagopus
19–24in/48–61cm

Identification A typical buteo, with broad wings and medium-length, white tail, with broad terminal band. Black belly and dark carpal patches are the best field marks. There is much plumage variation and dark birds may show only the characteristic tail. Hovers more than most buteos and soars on flat wings.
Voice Whistling.
Habitat Tundra and thin forests; winters on marshes.
Range Tundra Canada.
Movements Migrates to winter over most of the US except the extreme south. Migrant through temperate Canada.

Ferruginous Hawk

Buteo regalis 22–25in/56–64cm

Identification This is the largest of the buteos and is typically a western bird of arid brush country. Mottled in buffs and browns, but with rufous at bend of wing, on uppertail band and on legs. Rare, dark phase birds are brown with white flight feathers and all-white tail. Pale phase birds are white below, with only rufous patches on carpals, legs and tail.
Voice Raucous cries.
Habitat Open brush, prairies.
Range Breeds either side of the border in western Canada and US.
Movements Canadian birds move southwards to winter in western US and beyond.

Red-tailed Hawk

Buteo jamaicensis 19–25in/48–64cm

Identification The typical phase is brown above and paler below, with a narrow dark band across the belly and a plain rufous tail. A dark phase has brown body and wing linings contrasting with pale primaries. There is much plumage variation including birds with white tails. Young birds have finely-barred, brown tails. Harlan's Hawk is regarded as a phase of this species.
Voice High-pitched *kee-argh.*
Habitat Virtually any open area with adjacent woods – very widespread.
Range Virtually everywhere in North America except open tundra.
Movements Most Canadian birds move south in winter.

Red-shouldered Hawk

Buteo lineatus 15½–24in/40–61cm

Identification Well-marked buteo with rusty 'shoulders'. Upperparts brown, underparts closely barred rufous. In the air the upperwing is clearly banded black and white across the flight feathers, and the tail is equally clearly barred with broad black and narrow white bands. Below, the rusty body and wing linings contrast with pale flight feathers and the tail is barred black and white as above. Longer and more slender wings than Red-tailed Hawk.

Voice Screams.

Habitat Wet woodland.

Range Breeds over most of eastern US and into neighboring Canada. Also in California.

Movements North-eastern part of range abandoned in winter.

Swainson's Hawk

Buteo swainsoni

17½–22in/45–56cm

Identification A large buteo that makes the longest of migrations. Brown above and white below, marked by a broad, brown breast band. The tail is white, finely barred, and with a broad subterminal black band. A dark phase is brown below with no obvious breast band, but retains the pale tail pattern. Migrates in great swirling flocks.

Voice Whistle.

Habitat Plains, prairies, open grasslands.

Range From Alaska southwards through most of western and central US.

Movements Migrates south as far as Argentina, but some birds move across the US to winter in Florida.

Harris' Hawk

Parabuteo unicinctus

18–22in/46–56cm

Identification Adult is dark gray on body with rust-red 'shoulders', 'thighs' and, in flight, wing linings. The tail has a white base, a broad black band, is narrowly tipped white and is considerably longer than most other buteos.
Voice A scream.
Habitat Scrub, mesquite, brushland, semi-desert.
Range Penetrates US in south-west.
Movements Resident.

Zone-tailed Hawk

Buteo albonotatus

18½–22½in/47–55cm

Identification A very dark, virtually black buteo marked by black and white barred flight feathers, from below, and by a black and white barred tail. There are two or three clear-cut black bands on the tail – the similar, but rarer, Black Hawk, has only one broad, black tail band.
Voice Loud whistles.
Habitat Scrub and semi-desert.
Range Arizona, New Mexico and western Texas.
Movements May move across border into Mexico.

Golden Eagle

Aquila chrysaetos

30–35½in/76–90cm

Identification Huge, magnificient eagle which could be confused only with Bald Eagle in juvenile plumage. Adult is brown above and below, with wash of 'gold' on crown and nape. Juvenile and immatures have white base to tail and white bar along underwing. Soars on huge flat wings, glides over hillsides. Eagles have large prominent heads compared with buteos.
Voice Quiet mewing – mostly silent.
Habitat Tundra, mountains.
Range Northern Canada and western US.
Movements Northern birds move southwards over much US.

Bald Eagle

Haliaeetus leucocephalus

30–43in/76–109cm

Identification Large brown eagle with white head and neck and white tail. Juveniles are all brown, but feathers of tail usually show white bases at centers. Large yellow bill.
Voice Loud yelping.
Habitat Coasts, rivers, lakes.
Range Once widespread now confined to Alaska, northern Canada, some remote areas of US, and Florida.
Movements Winters along Pacific coast and in eastern half of US.

Osprey

Pandion haliaetus

21–24½in/53–62cm

Identification Lightly-built, gray and white bird of prey that is a pure 'fisherman'. Gray-brown above with small white head marked by black eyestripe. Underparts white. In flight, shows black barring across white underwing and bold, black carpal patches. The wings are long and narrow and held arched, like a gull. Hovers and plunges to catch prey.
Voice High-pitched whistles.
Habitat Shorelines, estuaries, lakes, rivers.
Range Breeds over much of North America, though absent from central US.
Movements Winters California, Florida and southwards.

Gyr Falcon

Falco rusticolus 20–25in/51–64cm

Identification A bird of the high arctic that only rarely wanders to US. Three distinct color phases occur, as well as intermediate plumages. Long, pointed wings, shortish tail and streamline shape pick out as a falcon. Most spectacular is white phase which is white, lightly speckled black. A gray phase is very pale, but more heavily speckled black, especially above. A dark phase is slate-gray above and heavily speckled below. The latter resembles a Peregrine, but lacks a prominent moustache.
Voice Slow *ka-ka-ka*.
Habitat Tundra, cliffs; in winter mainly coastal.
Range Alaskan and Canadian tundra including the archipelago.
Movements Irregular movements south to just beyond US border.

Prairie Falcon

Falco mexicanus 17–20in/43–51cm

Identification Brown falcon of the west, that is common where found. Upperparts, brown, edged buffy to produce a 'scaled' appearance. Underparts, white streaked brown. Head shows narrow moustachial streak that is repeated toward rear of head. Pale crown. In flight, shows narrow black axillaries – armpits.
Voice Shrill *kree-kree-kree.*
Habitat Mountains, prairies.
Range The west from British Columbia to Mexico.
Movements Moves southward from northern half of North American range.

Peregrine Falcon

Falco peregrinus 15–18½in/38–48cm

Identification Medium-sized, powerful falcon. Slate-gray above, white below, closely barred black. The black moustache against a white 'face' is a prominent field mark. The wings are long and angular, the tail relatively short. Juvenile is brown and streaked, rather than barred, below.
Voice Loud *kek-kek-kek.*
Habitat Cliffs on coasts, rivers, mountains.
Range Virtually extirpated by pesticide poisoning. Confined to far north – some reintroductions.
Movements Northern birds migrate to winter through Canada and northern states.

Merlin

Falco columbarious

10½–12½in/27–32cm

Identification Small, stocky falcon that takes mainly small birds. Male is slate-gray above with striped breast and only a hint of a moustachial streak. Female is brown and similarly marked. Flies low over ground, perches openly at dawn and dusk waiting to hunt.
Voice *Ki-ki-ki* when breeding.
Habitat Open tundra, moors, mountains; plus coasts in winter.
Range Breeds from Alaska across Canada and southwards through the Rockies.
Movements Migrates southwards to western, eastern and southern states.

American Kestrel

Falco sparverius

9–11in/23–28cm

Identification A dainty, well-marked falcon, common over much of North America. Male has rusty, black-barred back with dark blue inner wings. The head is boldly marked with patches of rust, white and black. The rusty tail is long and banded black at tip. Female is browner, with more barring and has only a rudimentary head pattern. Frequently hovers.
Voice High-pitched *kee-kee-kee.*
Habitat Open country.
Range Breeds everywhere except tundra.
Movements Canadian and mountain birds move southwards.

Aplomado Falcon

Falco femoralis

15–18in/38–46cm

Identification Medium-sized falcon of the extreme south. Adult is well marked with slate-gray upperparts, black belly and rusty legs and undertail. The white breast stands out at a distance and a closer approach reveals pale eyebrow. The long tail is banded black and white.
Voice Repeated *ka-ka-ka.*
Habitat Desert and dry grassland.
Range Rare along Mexican border.
Movements Wanders in breeding area.

Common Turkey

Meleagris gallopavo 36–48in/91–122cm

Identification Large ground bird with blue and red head wattles, iridescent black plumage and large tail, fanned in display.
Voice Loud gobbling.
Habitat Woodland clearings, scrub.
Range Scattered through US, once more widespread.
Movements Resident.

Blue Grouse

Dendragapus obscurus 15–21in/39–53cm

Identification Large grouse of woodland. Male is uniform gray below with white mottled flanks and brown upperparts. The tail is square and mainly dark. Female is brown with barring on foreparts and a boldly spotted belly. The dark tail is a useful feature.
Voice Booming calls of male.
Habitat Forests.
Range Breeds western states in mountains and near coast.
Movements Resident.

Spruce Grouse

Dendragapus canadensis 15–17in/38–43cm

Identification Common grouse of conifer forests. Male has black chin enclosed by white border and black on breast and central belly. There is a red wattle above the eye. Female heavily barred, but with black tail tipped rufous.
Voice Low-pitched booming.
Habitat Conifer forests.
Range Boreal zone from Alaska to Nova Scotia.
Movements Resident.

Ruffed Grouse

Bonasa umbellus 16–19in/41–48cm

Identification Secretive bird of forest edges. There are two color phases: red and gray. 'Red' birds are rufous above with brown barring below. The tail is large and heavily banded rust and black. 'Gray' birds are gray rather than rusty. Both phases have a dark mark on the side of the neck and fan their tail in flight and in display on a hollow log.
Voice Drumming sound produced by beating wings.
Habitat Forests, both deciduous and conifer.
Range The boreal zone extending southwards in Rockies and Appalachians and elsewhere.
Movements Resident.

Sharp-tailed Grouse

Tympanuchus phasianellus 15–20in/38–51cm

Identification Grassland grouse. Rather dully colored in shades of buff and brown in both sexes. Tail is pointed, larger in the male, and is fanned in display, when male shows violet patch on neck.
Voice Cooing in courtship.
Habitat Clearings in forest, open country.
Range Breeds from Alaska through north, west and central Canada as far east as Hudson's Bay and southwards into the prairies.
Movements Resident.

Sage Grouse

Centrocercus urophasianus

22–30in/56–76cm

Identification Largest of the grouse. Male is mottled buff and black above, and marked by black on throat, breast and belly, below. Most of the breast is whitish and, in display, this is puffed up and shows two yellow air sacs. The long tail is fanned to show a series of spikes. The female is smaller, duller, but also has a black belly.
Voice Popping sounds by male in display.
Habitat Arid sage brush country, plains.
Range From British Columbia to Nevada.
Movements Resident.

Willow Ptarmigan

Lagopus lagopus 11–17in/28–43cm

Identification Stocky grouse of open country. Male is rich rufous, with red comb and white wings and feet. In winter, whole plumage becomes white, when confusion with closely-related Rock Ptarmigan is likely.
Voice Crowing *koc-koc-koc*.
Habitat Tundra, open moors.
Range Alaska, northernmost Canada to Newfoundland.
Movements Some birds move south a short distance in winter.

Rock Ptarmigan

Lagopus mutus 13–14in/33–36cm

Identification Similar to Willow Ptarmigan, but mottled gray rather than red. Also white in winter, but dark mark between bill and eye creates an 'angry' expression.
Voice A rolling *karr.*
Habitat Found at higher altitudes and higher latitudes than Willow Ptarmigan; tundra and mountain tops.
Range Extreme north Canada and archipelago from Alaska to Newfoundland.
Movements Some southward movement in winter.

White-tailed Ptarmigan

Lagopus leucurus 12–13in/30–33cm

Identification Smaller than other ptarmigan. Similar to Rock Ptarmigan being mottled gray with white below and white wings. In flight, shows white, not black, tail and in winter is pure white with no dark mark between bill and eye. Thus even in winter the white tail is diagnostic.
Voice Low chuckle.
Habitat Mountain slopes.
Range From Alaska southwards through the Rockies to New Mexico.
Movements Resident.

Scaled Quail

Callipepla squamata 10–12in/25–30cm

Identification A distinctive western quail with a pale crest that gives it its country name of 'cotton-top'. Gray-brown above, rufous below and heavily 'scaled' over most of foreparts. Gregarious, runs rather than flies.
Voice A twanging *be-cos, be-cos.*
Habitat Semi-desert.
Range South-west US.
Movements Resident.

California Quail

Callipepla californica 9–11in/23–28cm

Identification One of series of western quails. Male is boldly marked with black and white on head, has a chocolate crown and a 'comma' shaped crest. The breast is blue and the underparts heavily barred. The latter, in both male and more subdued female, is best means of distinguishing from very similar Gambel's Quail.
Voice Loud *ka-ka-kow*.
Habitat Chaparral, brush, scrub.
Range Washington to Baja California.
Movements Resident.

Gambel's Quail

Callipepla gambelii 10–12in/26–30cm

Identification Very similar to California Quail, but found in drier, near desert country. Face pattern, crest and blue breast as California Quail, but underparts creamy with bold black patch on belly. Female lacks black patch.
Voice Similar to California Quail, but shorter.
Habitat Desert scrub.
Range South-western US.
Movements Resident.

Mountain Quail

Orcortyx pictus 10½–11½in/27–29cm

Identification Resembles other western quails, but foreparts less boldly patterned, with blue on breast extending over nape and crown. Chestnut bib enclosed by white, crest longer and straighter. Rusty belly shows bold pattern of white spots on flank.
Voice Low *whook*.
Habitat Arid mountain slopes.
Range South-western US.
Movements Resident, but leaves higher slopes in winter.

Montezuma Quail

Cyrtonyx montezumae 8–9½in/20–24cm

Identification Small, dark, chunky quail. Male is dark, chocolate-brown below, heavily spotted white on flanks. Head shows intricate pattern of interlaced black and white lines. Female, brown and buff with broken dark lines extending from eye to enclose chin.
Voice Soft whistling.
Habitat Evergreen forest floors.
Range South-western US.
Movements Resident.

Northern Bobwhite

Colinus virginianus 8–11in/20–28cm

Identification Virtually the only small gamebird that is at all common in the eastern US. Male is brown above, scaled white below, with distinctive white face enclosed by black. Female is similar, but has creamy face and less black. Best located by call.
Voice Distinctive *bob-white*.
Habitat Grasslands, farms.
Range Virtually the eastern half of the US to foothills of Rocky Mountain system. Introduced in the west.
Movements Resident.

Common Pheasant

Phasianus colchicus

20½–35½in/52–90cm

Identification Large colorful gamebird introduced from Europe. Male boldly colored in rich browns and golds, liberally spotted and barred in black and white. Blue head with bare red area around eye, often white neck-ring. Female subdued shades of brown and buff, with paler area around eye. Both sexes have long, pointed tails.
Voice Deep, resonant crowing.
Habitat Fields, thickets, woodland edges.
Range Widespread across northern US and southern Canada.
Movements Resident.

Chukar Partridge

Alectoris chukar 13–15in/33–39cm

Identification Substantial gamebird with distinctive face pattern of black enclosing a creamy bib. Bold series of black and white stripes along flanks. Red legs and bill.
Voice Distinct *choo-kar* repeated.
Habitat Arid mountain scrub.
Range High plateau of Rocky Mountain system. Introduced from Europe.
Movements Resident.

Gray Partridge

Perdix perdix 11½–12½in/29–32cm

Identification Chunky gamebird with orange face, brown streaked upperparts and gray breast. Underparts show smudgy chestnut 'horseshoe'. Gregarious bird of open areas.
Voice A fast *krikri-kri-kri-krikri.*
Habitat Fields, grasslands.
Range Either side of US-Canada border right across the continent. Introduced from Europe.
Movements Resident.

Common Egret

Egretta alba 35–41in/89–104cm

Identification Largest, all-white egret marked by large yellow bill and dark legs. Neck mostly held in distinctly kinked manner when at rest. The white form of the Great Blue Heron found in Florida is larger and has gray-green legs.
Voice Croaks.
Habitat Marshes, pools, estuaries.
Range Breeds over much of the US except the grassland and mountain interior.
Movements Moves southward to winter on south-eastern, Gulf and southern Pacific coasts.

Snowy Egret

Egretta thula 20–27in/51–68cm

Identification Slim, elegant egret with white plumage, black bill, black legs and yellow feet. When feeding in mud the feet may appear black, even in flight afterwards. Young Little Blue Heron is also white, but has heavier gray bill and paler legs.
Voice Mostly silent.
Habitat Marshes, lake margins, estuaries.
Range Widespread over western, eastern and southern states.
Movements Migrates southward in winter to South America, though some overwinter in California and from Florida north to South Carolina.

Cattle Egret

Bubulcus ibis 19–21in/48–53cm

Identification Small, robust, white egret that associates with domestic animals and agricultural machinery. Neck mostly held tucked into shoulders; upright walking stance; yellow bill and black legs. In breeding season bill becomes orange, legs become pink and there is a warm wash of buff on head, back and breast.
Voice Usually silent.
Habitat Marshes, grasslands, arable.
Range Colonist this century from Old World. Has spread northwards through southern and eastern states as far as New England. Has been recorded in eastern Canada.
Movements Largely resident.

Great Blue Heron

Ardea herodias

39–52in/99–132cm

Identification Large, mainly gray heron with white head marked by fine black crest. Pale, streaked foreneck. Flies on huge arched, dark wings with neck tucked back in 'shoulders'.
Voice Harsh squawks.
Habitat Ponds, lakes, marshes, estuaries.
Range Widespread resident over most of temperate North America.
Movements Northern birds move southwards in winter.

Green Heron

Butorides striatus 15–22in/38–56cm

Identification Small, bittern-like heron of dense thickets and aquatic vegetation. Adult has chestnut face, neck and breast with dark green upperparts. There is a black crest and it has reddish legs. Usually seen flying on rounded wings between one patch of cover and another like dark Least Bittern.
Voice Sharp croaks.
Habitat Marshes and lake margins with dense vegetation.
Range Breeds in western and eastern states, absent from prairies and Rockies.
Movements Winters southern California and Florida, otherwise migratory from remainder of range.

Black-crowned Night Heron

Nycticorax nycticorax 23–28in/58–71cm

Identification A crepuscular heron most active at dawn and dusk. Always holds itself hunched up, disguising its length of neck. Adult has black crown and back, gray wings and white underparts. The bill is decidedly chunky, the legs a yellow-orange. Immatures are streaked in a gray-buff. In flight, the chunky effect is enforced.
Voice Various croaks.
Habitat Flooded thickets, riversides.
Range Breeds over much of US northwards into southern Canada.
Movements Winters in west and east, including Mississippi River system.

American Bittern

Botaurus lentiginosus
23–34in/58–86cm

Identification Large, round-winged heron that skulks among reeds beds and is usually seen briefly in flight. Whole plumage streaked in buffs and browns with a dark cap and broad dark moustachial streak. Bill is large and yellow, legs green. When caught in open, tries to merge with imaginary marsh-type vegetation.
Voice A booming *onk-a-sonk.*
Habitat Marshes.
Range Breeds across southern Canada and much of US.
Movements Leaves northern and central parts of range in winter.

Least Bittern

Ixobrychus exilis 11–14in/28–35cm

Identification Very small heron that clings to tops of bushes or reeds, but spends most of its time inside deep cover. Male has black crown and back with bold, warm, buffy wing patches, that are particularly obvious in flight. Female and immature similar, but more dully colored.
Voice Quiet coo-ing.
Habitat Marshes, reed-beds.
Range Absent from prairies and mountains, otherwise widely spread across US.
Movements Migratory wintering only in Florida, southern Texas and southern California.

American Wood Stork

Mycteria americana

40–44in/102–112cm

Identification Still widely called 'Wood Ibis'. Large white bird with bare, black head and upper neck, and long, thick decurving black bill. The long legs trail prominently in flight when the white body and wing linings contrast with the flight feathers. Soars like other storks and nests in large colonies.
Voice Croaks when breeding.
Habitat Marshes with trees.
Range Breeds from Gulf Coast to Florida and north to South Carolina.
Movements Winters Florida.

White-faced Glossy Ibis

Plegadis chihi

22–25in/56–63cm

Identification A bronzy-purple, glossy-plumaged bird, with long legs, long neck and long decurved bill. Very similar to Glossy Ibis, but with bold white line around the eye and bill to form an enclosed area in summer. When this white area is lost in winter it becomes virtually impossible to separate from Glossy Ibis.
Voice Quacking calls.
Habitat Marshes with thickets and reeds.
Range From California inland to Idaho and along Texas and Louisiana coasts.
Movements Winters Mexico and southern California.

Sandhill Crane

Grus canadensis

34–48in/86–122cm

Identification Gray crane, with droopy gray 'tail' and red topped crown. Like other cranes, flies with neck extended.
Voice Loud rolling rattle.
Habitat Marshes, ponds and tundra.
Range Breeds over large areas of Canadian and Alaskan tundra as well as on prairies westwards to Pacific coast. Also in Florida.
Movements Spectacular migrations southward to Mexico, California and Texas. Resident Florida.

Virginia Rail

Rallus limicola

9–11in/23–28cm

Identification Colorful, long-billed rail. Upperparts streaked black and brown, underparts warm rust with undertail black, finely barred white. Legs reddish; bill reddish, slightly decurved. Immature is dusky, streaked gray and black, with black and white barred undertail. Skulking and seldom seen.
Voice Characteristic *kickit-kickit-kickit.*
Habitat Marshes with dense vegetation.
Range Breeds right across US, save for southern states, northwards into Canada.
Movements Winters Pacific coast, Florida and Gulf and Atlantic coasts.

Sora Rail

Porzana carolina 8–10in/20–25cm

Identification Common but secretive rail. Adult is streaked brown above and plain gray below, with black and white striped undertail. A dark crown, black 'face' and central breast make identification easy, if seen. Bill and legs yellow. Immature has dusky face, yellow bill, green legs.

Voice A pleasant, descending trill.
Habitat Marshes.
Range Throughout northern US and southern Canada.
Movements Winters California, Gulf and Atlantic coasts and Florida. Most birds leave North America.

Yellow Rail

Coturnicops noveboracensis 6–8in/15–20cm

Identification Small buff and brown rail marked by yellow legs and bill and smudgy, dark mark through eye. Banded on undertail coverts. Shows bold white patch on trailing edge of inner wing when flushed.
Voice Click notes in series of twos and threes – like tapping two stones together.
Habitat Floods, damp grasslands.
Range Breeds across much of central and eastern Canada, as well as in adjacent areas across the US border.
Movements Winters California, Gulf and Atlantic coasts and Florida.

Black Rail

Laterallus jamaicensis 5–6in/13–15cm

Identification Tiny black rail that mainly frequents brackish coastal marshes. Foreparts blue-black; back and hindparts black with fine white vertical bars. Patch of chestnut at top of back. Bill short and conical. Very difficult to see.
Voice High pitched *kic-ki-doo,* the last note being quieter and lower pitched.
Habitat Salt, brackish and sometimes fresh marshes.
Range Breeds both Pacific and Atlantic coasts and in some places inland.
Movements Winters Florida and Gulf Coast.

Clapper Rail

Rallus longirostris 14–15½in/35–40cm

Identification A large pale rail, similar to King Rail, but largely confined to salt marshes. Upperparts gray-brown, lightly streaked; underparts gray on breast, banded gray and white on flanks and undertail. Bill long and yellowish, legs pinkish.
Voice Loud *kek-kek-kek-kek*.
Habitat Saltmarsh.
Range Most coasts of US, though less continuous along rocky Pacific.
Movements Resident.

Common Gallinule

Gallinula chloropus 12–14in/31–35cm

Identification Medium-sized waterbird that swims well and is often confiding, even tame. Back is dark brown separated from the black underparts by a bold white, flank slash. The undertail is white and frequently cocked when walking. The remaining plumage is black with a bold, red, frontal shield. The legs are green-yellow, with long toes; the bill red, tipped yellow.
Voice Loud *currick*.
Habitat Pond and lake margins.
Range Breeds over most of eastern US and in Pacific Coast area.
Movements Migrates southwards to Gulf and Atlantic coasts.

American Coot

Fulica americana 14–15in/35–39cm

Identification All-black waterbird that spends much time swimming. Runs over water to avoid danger and may then show white trailing edge to the wing. Otherwise white bill and frontal shield, plus white outer feathers of undertail coverts are the best field marks.
Voice Sharp *kuk-kuk-kuk.*
Habitat Ponds, lakes, coastal bays.
Range Breeds over most of temperate North America northwards into the Canadian prairies.
Movements Leaves interior in winter.

American Black Oystercatcher

Haematopus bachmani 17–17½in/43–45cm

Identification All-black shorebird of stout build, with large red bill and pink legs.
Voice Loud *wee-wee-wee*.
Habitat Rocky shorelines.
Range Pacific coast from Alaska to Baja California.
Movements Resident.

American Avocet

Recurvirostra americana

16–20in/41–51cm

Identification Slim, elegant shorebird with long blue legs and black recurved bill. Feeds with side-to-side motion, sifting soft mud. Black and white plumage with rusty wash on head and neck.

Voice Loud *kleep.*
Habitat Fresh and saline lakes.
Range Breeds western half of US northwards into Canada.
Movements Moves to coasts in winter.

Black-winged Stilt

Himantopus himantopus

13–16in/33–41cm

Identification Often called Black-necked Stilt, but now regarded as conspecific with Old World birds. Extremely long-legged wader; black above, white below with long neck and needle-like bill. Pink legs trail in flight.
Voice Loud repeated *keep-keep.*
Habitat Fresh and saline pools and shallow marshes.
Range Western US and, in the south, along the Gulf Coast to Florida.
Movement Migrant, but winters California.

Mountain Plover

Charadrius montanus

8–9½in/20–24cm

Identification Brown plover with white underparts in summer. Sandy smudges at sides of breast, black crown, white forehead and eyebrow are main features. In winter, face and breast are washed sandy. White wing-bar and tail margins in flight.
Voice *Krrr* in flight.
Habitat Grassy plains at altitude.
Range Breeds through eastern foothills of Rockies.
Movements Moves southward to winter, but regular as far north as California.

Pacific Golden Plover

Pluvialis fulva 9–10in/23–26cm

Identification Very similar to American Golden Plover, but smaller, slimmer and with shorter wings than that bird. Tends to be more coastal. Pale, more pronounced eyebrow may be first clue to identification.
Voice Fast *teu-ee*.
Habitat Tundra, grassland.
Range Breeds western Alaska.
Movements Migrates westwards to Hawaii and Oceana.

Black-bellied Plover

Pluvialis squatarola

11–12in/28–31cm

Identification Similar to golden plovers, but in all plumages spangled black and white above. In summer 'face' and belly are black, bordered by white line. In winter, underparts mottled gray. Shows white wing bar and black axillaries (arm pits) in flight.
Voice Whistled *tlee-oo-ee.*
Habitat Tundra; in winter, estuaries and shorelines.
Range Breeds far northern Alaska and Canada.
Movements Migrates to winter all coasts as far north as Washington and New England.

Snowy Plover

Charadrius alexandrinus

6–6½in/15–17cm

Identification Small sandy plover marked in summer and winter by dark marks at sides of breast. Immature shows no more than a smudge. Legs black. Wing-bar and white, outer tail show in flight.
Voice *Wit-wit-wit.*
Habitat Sandy wastes and margins of saline and fresh marshes, open shorelines.
Range Breeds locally throughout the west, and along the Pacific Coast.
Movements Migrates southward and to the Pacific Coast to winter.

Semipalmated Plover

Charadrius semipalmatus $6\frac{1}{2}$–8in/17–20cm

Identification Common along shorelines. Brown above and white below marked by neat head pattern of black and white, and bold, black breast band. Orange bill tipped black; orange or yellowish legs.
Voice Pleasant *chur-lee.*
Habitat Breeds tundra; winters, sandy shores and estuaries.
Range Alaskan and Canadian tundra.
Movements Migrates to winter in California and along Atlantic and Gulf coasts.

Killdeer

Charadrius vociferus

9–11in/23–28cm

Identification Common and widespread plover of fields and grasslands. Easily picked out by black face pattern and double, black breast bands. Rusty rump and pointed tail most visible in flight.
Voice *Kill-dee,* repeated.
Habitat Fields and grasslands.
Range Breeds throughout US and temperate Canada.
Movements Leaves northern and central parts of range in winter.

Long-billed Curlew

Numenius americanus 20–26in/51–66cm

Identification Unmistakable, large, brown shorebird with huge, decurved bill. Young birds have shorter bills. Cinnamon underwing is diagnostic.
Voice Clear *coo-lee.*
Habitat Prairies in summer; winters on estuaries, shorelines.
Range Western states from high plateaux to upland prairies extending northwards into Canada and south to Texas.
Movements Migrates south to western Gulf Coast and California.

Whimbrel

Numenius phaeopus 15–17in/39–43cm

Identification Large shorebird with striped crown and longish decurved bill. Similar to Long-billed Curlew, but smaller, shorter bill curves more toward the tip. Rare Bristle-thighed Curlew of west Alaska is very similar, but has rusty rump.
Voice Seven high pitched whistles form a trill.
Habitat Tundra, shorelines and marshes in winter.

Range Breeds coastal Alaska and Canadian arctic.
Movements Migrates mostly along coasts to winter in California and Florida.

Marbled Godwit

Limosa fedoa

16–20in/41–51cm

Identification Large, long-billed, long-legged shorebird. Brown spangled with black and white above; buff, barred brown below. Long pinkish bill, tipped black and slightly uptilted. Legs gray, trail in flight. No prominent marks in flight. *See* Hudsonian Godwit.

Voice *Kar-rack.*

Habitat Grasslands; in winter, near coasts or along shorelines.

Range Prairies of US-Canada border.

Movements Migrates southward to winter in California and Gulf Coast.

Hudsonian Godwit

Limosa haemastica

14–15in/36–39cm

Identitication Smaller than Marbled Godwit and marked at all times by black and white rump and tail pattern, and white wing-bar. In summer, chestnut breast is closely barred black. In winter, is brown above and buff below.

Voice *Quit-quit.*

Habitat High arctic tundra, estuaries in winter.

Range Northernmost Canada to western shores of Hudson's Bay.

Movements Passes out over Atlantic on way to South American wintering grounds. Returns via Central Flyway.

Upland Sandpiper

Bartramia longicauda

11–12½in/28–32cm

Identification A shorebird that is most at home on grassland. Streaked brown and black above, streaked and arrowed brown below, with contrasting white belly. Long yellow legs, long thin neck with curiously emaciated look to head. Medium-length, thin bill and long, wedge-shaped tail. The shape, buffy coloration and habitat preference make this an easily identified bird.

Voice *Quip-ip-ip-ip.*

Habitat Grasslands.

Range From Alaska through prairies eastwards to the Great Lakes, the mid-west and Maine.

Movements Leaves North America to winter.

Buff-breasted Sandpiper

Tryngites subruficollis 7½– 8½in/19–21cm

Identification Uniformly warm-buff underparts and plain face pick this bird out easily. Upperparts darkly streaked, thin bill, yellow legs.

Voice *Preeet.*

Habitat Breeds tundra, passage and winter on short-grass meadows and fields.

Range Breeds only north Canadian arctic west of Hudson's Bay to north-east Alaska.

Movements Fall, migrant on east coast; winters Argentina.

Solitary Sandpiper

Tringa solitaria

8–8½in/20–22cm

Identification A bird of ponds and streams rather than open marshes and estuaries. Taller, slimmer and more elegant than Spotted Sandpiper. Upperparts very dark, liberally spotted white. Streaked on sides of neck, breast, and lightly barred on flanks. Long neck, rounded head, medium length thin bill. Legs long and black, trail beyond tail in flight. Dark rump, black and white barred tail and uniform dark wings show in flight. Several other dark sandpipers have white rump.

Voice *Weet-weet-weet.*

Habitat Ponds, streams, breeds on boggy pools.

Range Mainly boreal zone from Alaska across Canada.

Movements Winters southwards in Central and South America.

Spotted Sandpiper

Actitis macularia

7½in/19cm

Identification Brown above, white below, evenly spotted with black in summer. In winter, underparts are white and best field mark is wedge of white between breast and wing. Bobs body continuously, flies low on jerky wings.

Voice High-pitched *weet-weet.*

Habitat Running streams, ponds, lakesides, marshes.

Range Breeds over most of North America except extreme tundra and all southern US.

Movements Winters Florida, Texas and California southwards.

Wandering Tattler

Heteroscelus incanus 10½–11½in/27–29cm

Identification In summer this is a gray bird, uniform above, heavily barred below. In winter the barring disappears and the breast and flanks are gray, the belly white. At all seasons the legs are yellow, the bill medium and thick based. In flight, the upperparts show no wing bar or tail pattern.
Voice Rapid whistles.
Habitat Breeds mountains; winters, rocky shorelines.
Range Mountains of Alaska.
Movements Migrates to winter around Pacific including California.

Willet

Catoptrophorus semipalmatus 14–17in/36–43cm

Identification A large gray shorebird that is heavily barred and streaked in summer, but gray and white in winter. Strong gray legs and long, somewhat thickly-based bill give an impression of solidity. Black and white wings diagnostic at all times.
Voice *Pee-wee-wee.*
Habitat Damp grasslands and pond shores; winters on lagoons, estuaries.
Range Breeds in central Rockies and northern prairies into Canada.
Movements Migrates to all coasts to winter and into South America.

Greater Yellowlegs

Tringa melanoleuca

12½–15in/32–38cm

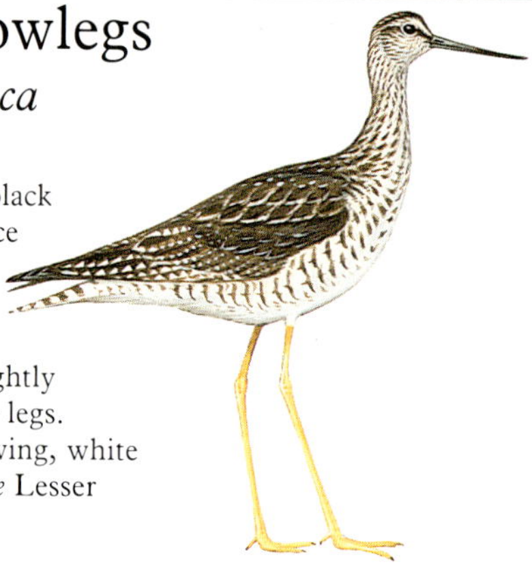

Identification Mottled black and white above to produce a gray impression; white below with some streaking on neck and breast. Long, thickish, slightly upturned bill; long yellow legs. In flight, shows uniform wing, white rump and trailing legs. *See* Lesser Yellowlegs.
Voice Loud *keu-keu-keu.*
Habitat Breeds between boreal and tundra zones – taiga; winters fresh marshes, lakes.
Range Breeds in band from southern Alaska to Newfoundland.
Movements Winters across southern US and along all three coasts, southwards to South America.

Lesser Yellowlegs

Tringa flavipes

9½–11in/24–28cm

Identification Superficially similar to Greater Yellowlegs, but much more lightly and more elegantly built. Gray above, white below, but with longer neck, smaller head, pencil-thin straight bill. Legs yellow and proportionately longer. Uniform wing and white rump in flight.
Voice *Yoo-yoo.*
Habitat Tundra and taiga marshes and bogs in summer; winters fresh marshes.
Range More northerly than Greater Yellowlegs from Alaska and Canadian arctic to Hudson's Bay.
Movements Winters, Gulf Coast and Florida southwards.

Stilt Sandpiper

Micropalama himantopus

8–8½in/20–22cm

Identification In summer, brown above with heavily and completely barred underparts. Also chestnut eye stripe and ear coverts. In winter, is gray above and white below with clear dark eyestripe. At all times, long grayish legs and long, slightly drooping bill are useful, giving the bird a peculiar, if not unique, shape. White rump shows in flight.
Voice *Tu-tu.*
Habitat Tundra in summer; freshwater shores in winter.
Range Breeds on central Canadian tundra.
Movements Winters South America.

Short-billed Dowitcher

Limnodromus griseus

10–12in/26–30cm

Identification Very similar to Long-billed Dowitcher and to be distinguished at all seasons with the greatest of care. These are chunky, large-bodied waders that have long, straight bills and feed with a vigorous probing motion. In summer they are spangled chestnut and black above; chestnut with bars and spots below. The length of bill is of little value in the field and there is considerable overlap. In flight, both species show a narrow white wing-bar on the secondaries and a white 'V' extending up the rump. Both have green legs. The main differences are that the present species has a white tail with narrow black bars, whereas the Long-billed has a black tail with narrow white bars. Additionally, the present species has black chestnut striped tertials in summer and autumn, including juveniles.
Voice Melodic *tu-tu-tu.*
Habitat Boreal marshes; winters, estuaries.
Range Breeds coastal Alaska, central northern Canada.
Movements Winters all coasts southwards of California and South Carolina.

Long-billed Dowitcher

Limnodromus scolopaceus 10½–12½in/27–32cm

Identification A chunky, long-billed shorebird, very similar to Long-billed Dowitcher. For distinctions see that species. Generally darker, with a darker tail than that bird.
Voice Shrill *keek*.
Habitat Tundra bogs; winters found more often on fresh marshes than Short-billed.
Range Breeds western Alaska and adjacent north coast of Canada.
Movements Winters, coastal US from Washington to Florida.

Surfbird

Aphriza virgata 9½–10in/24–26cm

Identification Robust, short-billed shorebird of rocky coastlines. Always appears plump with short orange bill tipped black, and short yellow legs. In summer is heavily spotted above and below. In winter, much duller with uniform gray 'face' and breast, like Purple Sandpiper. In flight, shows very bold, white wing-bar and white tail with black terminal band.
Voice Whistle of three notes.
Habitat Tundra mountains.
Range Breeds Alaska and neighboring Canada.
Movements Winters along Pacific Coast.

Ruddy Turnstone

Arenaria interpres

8½–9½in/22–24cm

Identification Stocky wader, found only along shorelines, with short, stubby bill and stone-turning habits. In summer, has a 'harlequin' 'face' pattern in black and white with rich chestnut and black wings. In winter, smudgy 'face' pattern and grayish upperparts; legs, short and red. In flight, shows white 'braces' and wing-bar.
Voice Sharp *tuk-a-tuk*.
Habitat Rocky and muddy coasts; breeds on tundra islands.
Range Far northern Canada and archipelago and coastal Alaska.
Movements Winters on all coasts of US.

Black Turnstone

Arenaria melanocephala 8½–9½in/22–24cm

Identification Similar in size, shape and habits to Ruddy Turnstone, but essentially a western bird. In summer, black above, white below with white spot between eye and bill. Dull sooty above in winter with uniform face. Boldly black and white in flight.
Voice As Ruddy Turnstone but higher.
Habitat Tundra coasts in summer; rocky coasts in winter.
Range Breeds western coastal Alaska.
Movements Winters Pacific Coasts.

Rock Sandpiper

Calidris ptilocnemis 8½–9½in/22–24cm

Identification The western equivalent of the east coast Purple Sandpiper. In summer, heavily spotted below with spots boldly merging on breast to form 'Dunlin-type' patch. In winter, head and breast uniformly dull gray.
Voice Repeated *ticker.*
Habitat Breeds tundra; winters rocky shores.
Range Breeds western Alaska.
Movements Winters west coasts as far south as northern California.

Pectoral Sandpiper

Calidris melanotos 7–8½in/18–21cm

Identification Stocky shorebird marked by large, plump body with short, thin neck and small head and shortish orange-yellow legs. In all plumages, shape, plus uniformly streaked neck and breast ending abruptly to form clear-cut pectoral band, are best field marks.
Voice Far carrying *kreet.*
Habitat Summer tundra; passage and winter fresh marshes, pond margins.
Range Breeds northern coasts of Alaska and Canada.
Movements Mainly a migrant, especially on east coast. Winters South America.

Red Knot

Calidris canutus 9½–10½in/24–27cm

Identification Stocky shorebird that may occur in large numbers at favored sites. In summer, underparts are pure chestnut. In winter, gray above, white below rather like large, rotund, short-billed Dunlin.
Voice Dull *nut*.
Habitat Arctic tundra; winters on shorelines and estuaries.
Range Central Canadian archipelago.
Movements Winters coasts of California, Gulf Coast, Florida and Atlantic.

Dunlin

Calidris alpina 6–7½in/16–19cm

Identification Stocky little shorebird marked by black belly in summer. In winter, gray above, white below with streaking on breast. In all plumages relatively long, slightly decurved bill is good feature. Juvenile is warm buffy above and on breast, but is always streaked.
Voice Nasal *tree*.
Habitat Breeds tundra; passage and winters coastal marshes, shorelines, estuaries.
Range Alaskan and Canadian tundra east to Hudson's Bay.
Movements Winters all coasts.

Sanderling

Calidris alba 7½–8½in/19–22cm

Identification A neat little shorebird, most often seen in small flocks running up and down beaches following the movements of the surf. In winter, pale gray plumage with black at bend of wing is diagnostic. In summer, rich chestnut head, back and breast are heavily spotted black. Shortish black bill.
Voice Rippling *kip-kip*.
Habitat Tundra; sandy beaches in winter.
Range Canadian archipelago.
Movements Winters along all coasts.

White-rumped Sandpiper

Calidris fuscicollis 6–7in/16–18cm

Identification Neat little shorebird with shortish black legs and short, straight bill. Slimline accentuated by long wings projecting beyond tail. Generally grayish, with streaking on breast extending as 'arrowheads' along flanks, particularly in breeding plumage. Juvenile has chestnut wash on back and crown. In flight shows white rump.
Voice Shrill *jeet*.
Habitat Tundra; passage and winters marshes and estuaries.
Range Northern and archipelago coasts of Alaska and Canada.
Movements Moves mainly south and east to winter in South America.

Baird's Sandpiper

Calidris bairdii

$6\frac{1}{2}-7\frac{1}{2}$in/17–19cm

Identification A short-legged, short-billed sandpiper with long wings accentuating slim, elongated appearance. In all plumages, warm, buffy wash over scaly upperparts and streaked breast creates impression of a 'brown' rather than 'gray' bird.
Voice Harsh *kreep.*
Habitat Tundra; on passage on marshes and pond-edges.
Range Breeds northern Alaska and Canada, extending northwards into the archipelago.
Movements Moves southwards through the Central Flyway to South America.

Least Sandpiper

Calidris minutilla $5-5\frac{1}{2}$in/13.5–14.5cm

Identification Tiny sandpiper with short, thin bill slightly downcurved and yellow legs: the latter may be muddy and appear dark. In summer and winter, breast-streaking forms a band; juvenile has buffy breast with streaking at sides. Scaly upperparts with rich, buffy feather margins; hint of pale inverted 'V' on back.
Voice High-pitched *kreep.*
Habitat Tundra; on passage and, in winter, marshes, pools, lagoons.
Range In summer from Alaska across arctic Canada to Labrador.
Movements On passage throughout North America to winter through southern states and along all coasts.

Semipalmated Sandpiper

Calidris pusilla 5½–6in/14–16cm

Identification Common, small shorebird with partially webbed feet that are virtually impossible to see in the field. Short, straight bill with thick base and blunt tip. Upperparts with feathers edged buff to create a regular, uniform pattern. This latter feature is important when comparing with easily confused Western Sandpiper.
Voice An abrupt *chirk*.
Habitat Tundra; on passage, marshes, pools, sheltered bays.
Range Breeds northern Alaska across Canada to Labrador.
Movements Passes through centre and east coast on way to South America to winter.

Western Sandpiper

Calidris mauri 6–6½in/15.5–17cm

Identification Of all the 'peep' (small sandpipers) this is the longest legged and longest billed, but it is still easy to confuse with Semipalmated Sandpiper. In summer, this bird has chestnut on crown, ear coverts and back and and is marked by extensive streaking on breast with 'arrow-like' markings on sides of neck and flanks. Juvenile has chestnut on scapulars and an irregular feather pattern on folded wings: compare with uniform scaly upperparts of Semipalmated. Also has less pronounced eyebrow.
Voice High-pitched *jeet*.
Habitat Breeds tundra; winters marshes, bays.
Range Breeds north and west coastal Alaska.
Movements Winters all coasts, often common on passage.

Wilson's Phalarope

Phalaropus tricolor 8½–10in/22–26cm

Identification Less inclined to swim than other phalaropes. In summer, female has bold chestnut 'S' extending from the eye, along the side of the neck to trail over the back. Male is similar, but duller and darker. In winter, pale gray above, white below with thin, needle-like bill 1½ times length of head. No black comma behind eye as in other phalaropes.

Voice A croak.

Habitat Marshes.

Range Breeds over much of western North America extending eastward through Great Lakes and increasing in eastern Canada.

Movements Winters in South America, moving southwards mainly along west coast.

Red Phalarope

Phalaropus fulicarius 7½–8½in/19–21cm

Identification A swimming shorebird that spends the winter at sea. In summer, rich chestnut underparts and white 'face' preclude confusion. In winter, gray above, white below with dark comma extending from eye. Bill, thick and yellow-based compared with other phalaropes' needle-thin ones.

Voice High *twit.*

Habitat Tundra, on passage along coasts; winters at sea.

Range Tundra coasts of Alaska, Canada and archipelago.

Movements Mostly seen on passage wind blown to coasts.

Red-necked Phalarope

Phalaropus lobatus 6½–7½in/17–19cm

Identification Small, delicate phalarope. In summer, gray with white chin and red neck patch. In winter, gray with black comma behind eye. Shortish, needle-like bill. Juvenile much darker above.
Voice Quiet *tit*.
Habitat Tundra pool; winters at sea.
Range Alaskan and Canadian tundra.
Movements Migrates along coasts to winter at sea.

Common Snipe

Gallinago gallinago

10–10½in/25–27cm

Identification Highly camouflaged marshland bird heavily streaked in brown, black and buff with bold, double 'V' in cream on back. Long, straight bill is probed vigorously while feeding. When flushed, towers with zig-zag flight into the air. Nuptial flight consists of series of aerial dives with stiff outertail feathers vibrating to produce a bleeting sound.
Voice Harsh *scarp*.
Habitat Wide variety of marshes.
Range Throughout Alaska and Canada, except northernmost tundra, southwards through northern US.
Movements Winters in east, west and southern states.

Parasitic Jaeger

Stercorarius parasiticus

15–19in/38–48cm

Identification Dark, athletic seabird that pursues other seabirds to rob them of food. In summer, adult has two extended tail feathers projecting in flight, but these are often broken by the fall. At all times this is a narrow-winged, angular jaeger that is smaller than Pomarine and heavier than Long-tailed. Pale phase birds have dark cap and pale underparts with ill-defined dark breast band. Dark phase birds are uniform brown. Both show white flashes in dark wings.
Voice High-pitched *kee-ow* on breeding grounds.
Habitat Arctic tundra; passage and winter and sea.
Range Breeds Alaska, Northern Canada and in archipelago.
Movements Migrates along west coast, less numerous off east coast, to winter at sea off South America.

Pomarine Jaeger

Stercorarius pomarinus

17–21in/43–53cm

Identification Summer adult has extended central tail feathers, blunt-tipped and twisted. In autumn, heavy build and, in pale phase birds, prominent breast band are best features. In all, plumages has more white in wing flashes than other jaegers.
Voice Silent at sea.
Habitat Tundra in summer; at sea in winter.
Range Breeds north coasts of Alaska, Canada and archipelago.
Movements Moves southward along west coast, rather scarce off east coast.

Long-tailed Jaeger

Stercorarius longicaudus

15–22in/38–56cm

Identification Smallest and most lightly built of the jaegers, more tern-like than others. Summer adult has long tail streamers. In fall, shows little, if any, white wing flash; but contrast between grayish upperparts and all-black flight feathers. Juvenile shows white wing flashes on under surface. At all times, size and build are best features.
Voice Silent at sea.
Habitat Summer, tundra; winter, sea.
Range Western and northern Alaska, northern Canada and archipelago; winters off South America.
Movements Scarcest of jaegers on passage, more regular west than east coast.

Great Skua

Stercorarius skua

22–24in/56–61cm

Identification Heavily-built, all-brown jaeger with broad wings marked by bold, white flash. Body has rufous wash and is heavily streaked, creating a subtle contrast with darker, more uniformly brown wings. South Polar Skua is rare, mainly in west, and is more uniformly dark gray-brown.
Voice Nasal *skeer.*
Habitat Bare hills in summer; winters at sea.
Range Breeds in northern Europe.
Movements Regular offshore, east coast on passage.

Glaucous Gull

Larus hyperboreus

23–27in/58–69cm

Identification Large, pale gray gull, with broadly white-tipped flight feathers, that lacks contrasting wing tip pattern of most other pale gulls. Adult has yellow bill with red spot and pink legs. Pale eye creates a fierce expression. Juvenile is spotted buffy, has pale, creamy wings and pink base to bill.
Voice Harsh *kyow.*
Habitat Breeds tundra; winters, coasts and some inland waters.
Range Breeds coastal Alaska, Canada and to Labrador.
Movements Winters ice-free coasts in east and west and among Great Lakes.

Glaucous-winged Gull

Larus glaucescens 23½–26in/60–66cm

Identification Large, west coast gull marked by gray mantle extending to wing tips, broken only by white terminal mirrors. Bill is yellow with red spot and decidedly deep and heavy. Juvenile has all-black bill like young Iceland, but is buffy across wings rather than creamy.
Voice Harsh *kyow*.
Habitat Tundra coasts.
Range Breeds coastal Alaska southwards along coasts of Canada.
Movements Alaskan birds move southwards. Winters Pacific Coast to Mexico.

Western Gull

Larus occidentalis 23½–25in/60–64cm

Identification Dark-backed gull with heavy yellow bill, spotted red, and pink legs. Southern birds are very dark, almost black with white terminal mirrors; northern birds are paler, but still very dark. Hybrids with Thayer's Gull are widespread and confusing. This is the western equivalent of the Great Black-backed.
Voice Loud *owk*.
Habitat Coasts.
Range West coast southwards from Vancouver.
Movements Resident.

Herring Gull

Larus argentatus

21½–23½in/54–60cm

Identification Gray-mantled, medium-sized gull with contrasting black wing tips marked by white mirrors. Bill, yellow with red spot, legs pink. Juvenile is mottled in shades of brown and, in flight, has pale inner primaries with dark terminal spots.
Voice Loud *kyow-kyow*.
Habitat Coasts.
Range Breeds over much of northern Canada. Alaska and extending southwards through the eastern US. Most abundant coastal gull in most areas.
Movements Winters along Pacific coasts of Canada and US, on Atlantic and Gulf coasts and inland on Great Lakes and southern and eastern US.

California Gull

Larus californicus

19½–21½in/50–54cm

Identification Like smaller, darker Herring Gull with less massive, more rounded head and yellow bill with black and red spots. Legs are greenish yellow. Gray mantle, black wing tips with white mirrors. Juvenile is dark with pinkish legs.

Voice Yelping *kyow.*

Habitat Breeds on inland marshes and lakes; winters, coast.

Range Breeds on prairies and plateaux in Rockies.

Movements Pacific Coast from southern British Columbia to Mexico.

Ring-billed Gull

Larus delawarensis 17–18½in/43–47cm

Identification Pale gray gull with black wing tips and white mirrors. Bill, yellow with clear black vertical bar; legs yellow. In winter, spotted on crown and nape. From second winter, eye is pale creating a fierce expression. Immature, brown with grayish legs and dark eye, may be difficult to separate from Mew Gull, but has larger bill and head and is more spotted.

Voice Loud *kyow.*

Habitat Marshes and lakes in summer; in winter also along coasts.

Range Breeds in prairies and plateaux of Rockies eastwards through Great Lakes.

Movements Winters all coasts and inland especially in southern and eastern states.

Mew Gull

Larus canus

15–17in/38–43cm

Identification Gray-backed gull with black wing tips and large white mirrors. Gentle appearance, with rounded head, smallish yellow bill and yellow legs. Immatures have pink bills with black tips and grayish legs. First winter birds can be confused with similar aged Ring-billed, but head and bill shape distinct.
Voice High-pitched *kee-ar*.
Habitat tundra marshes in summer; coasts in winter.
Range Breeds Alaska and north-western Canada.
Movements Winters Pacific Coast.

Heermann's Gull

Larus heermanni 18–20in/46–51cm

Identification Dusky, west coast gull. Adult in summer is dusky on back and wings, gray below with paler neck and white head. Bill is red, tipped black, legs black. In winter, head becomes gray streaked black. Immatures are dusky all over. In flight, adult shows gray tail with broad black terminal band.
Voice *Whee-oo*.
Habitat Breeds on offshore islands, winters coasts.
Range Breeds Pacific Coast of US.
Movements Winters California southwards.

Black-legged Kittiwake

Rissa tridactyla 15–17in/38–43cm

Identification Gray-backed gull with long, narrow wings and pure black wing tips. Legs black and short, bill yellow. In winter, adult has dark smudge on nape. Immature has black 'W' across wings and black bar across nape. Abundant at cliff breeding colonies.
Voice Repeated *kitti-waak.*
Habitat Cliffs in summer; at sea in winter.
Range Breeds Alaska, Canadian archipelago, Newfoundland and Gulf of St Lawrence.
Movements Disperses over northern Pacific and Atlantic, but regularly seen along both coasts.

Franklin's Gull

Larus pipixcan
13–14in/33–36cm

Identification Black-hooded, summer visitor to prairies. In summer, upperparts are slate-gray marked by white wing tips broken by line of black mirrors. Underwing, uniform silver. Red bill and legs; bold white eye-ring. In winter, has remnant hood, particularly noticeable on ear coverts; shows white eye-ring prominently. Immatures similar to winter adult, with white breast and brownish, mottled wing. Often hawks insects in air.
Voice High pitched chuckle.
Habitat Lakes and marshes.
Range Breeds prairies and upland grasslands.
Movements Migrates through interior and Gulf Coast; rare winter visitor there and California.

Bonaparte's Gull

Larus philadelphia

12–13in/30–33cm

Identification Smallest regular gull marked by black head in summer and black spot behind the eye in winter. In flight, shows bold white forewing, both above and below, with trailing wing edge of black primary tips. Small black bill, short red legs.
Voice Chattering.
Habitat Tundra and muskeg ponds and marshes.
Range In broad band from Alaska through Canada almost to the Great Lakes.
Movements Winters, Great Lakes and all coasts of US.

Sabine's Gull

Xema sabini 12½–13½in/32–34cm

Identification Adult in summer has black outer primaries, white inner primaries and secondaries, contrasting with warm gray wing coverts and forming a unique flight pattern. Slate-gray hood, bordered by narrow black line, and black bill with yellow tip, are best features at rest, though primaries show white mirrors that are never obvious in flight. Hood lost in winter though some dusky on head and partial border remains. Black legs. Tail neatly notched. Flashes black and white in flight.
Voice Tern like.
Habitat Tundra coasts; winters at sea.
Range Western and northern coasts of Alaska, north and archipelago coasts of Canada.
Movements Reasonably common off Pacific Coast. Northern and eastern birds head eastwards over Atlantic to coasts of south-western Europe.

Least Tern

Sterna albifrons 9–10in/23–26cm

Identification Smallest tern marked by gray upperparts, white below with black cap and peaked white forehead. Bill and feet yellow, the former tipped black. Long narrow wings, frequently hovers, dives for food.
Voice High *ki-tik.*
Habitat Shorelines, beaches, sand bars.
Range Breeds all US coastlines and along Mississippi River system.
Movements Moves south in winter.

Arctic Tern

Sterna paradisaea

12–15in/30–39cm

Identification Summer adult is pale gray above and below with black cap and white cheeks. Bill is blood-red, legs short and red. Tail deeply forked. First winter has white trailing edge to inner wing. To be distinguished with care from Common Tern.
Voice *Key-rrr.*
Habitat Tundra marshes; winters at sea.
Range Breeds across whole of northern Canada and Alaska and, in the east, south to Nova Scotia.
Movements Long distance migrant to southern oceans.

Common Tern

Sterna hirundo

12–14in/30–36cm

Identification Pale gray above, paler below with black cap, but no contrasting white cheek patch. Bill orange-red with black tip (sometimes absent); legs orange-red. First winter, has dark trailing edge to wing contrasting with paler mid-wing panel. *See* Arctic Tern.
Voice High *kirri-kirri.*
Habitat Marshes, pools, lagoons, beaches.
Range Mainly across southern Canada eastwards of Rockies, but southwards across the US border.
Movements Winters on coasts of South America.

Forster's Tern

Sterna forsteri 13½–15in/34–38cm

Identification Like Common Tern, gray above and white below. Red bill with black tip; longer red legs. Tail, long and forked. In flight, shows white primaries and white edges to tail. In winter, black cap becomes bold black mark behind eye, bill all black.
Voice *Ky-aar.*
Habitat Marshes, scarce on coasts.
Range Breeds on prairies and plateaux among Rockies; also on Gulf Coast marshes and locally on Atlantic Coast.
Movements Winters, Gulf Coast, Florida, Atlantic Coast as far north as the Carolinas.

Gull-billed Tern

Gelochelidon nilotica 14–15in/35–39cm

Identification Large, pale gray tern with thick, bull-necked appearance and large, deep black bill. As pale as Sandwich Tern, but distinctive heavy shape. Legs black and long for a tern. Hawks insects over dry land and wetlands.
Voice Harsh *ka-wak.*
Habitat Coastal marshes.
Range Breeds, Atlantic and Gulf Coasts of US.
Movements Winters, Florida and Gulf Coast.

Elegant Tern

Sterna elegans 15½–17in/40–43cm

Identification Large gray tern with prominent ragged crest and long, thin orange-red to yellowish bill. Legs, black. In winter, crest starts at eye and extends over hind crown. *See* Royal Tern.
Voice Harsh *kee-rick.*
Habitat Coasts.
Range Breeds, coastal Mexico to Baja California.
Movements California coasts in fall.

Royal Tern

Sterna maxima 17½–20in/45–51cm

Identification Similar to Elegant Tern, but with thicker, orange-red bill. In winter, black crest starts behind (not at) black eye. Legs, black.
Voice High pitched *chirrip.*
Habitat Coasts.
Range Breeds on Gulf and Atlantic coasts.
Movements Winters, southern California, Gulf and Atlantic coasts and Florida.

Caspian Tern

Sterna caspia 19–22in/48–56cm

Identification Huge gray tern with massive coral red bill. Black cap in summer, mottled in winter. Legs long and black.
Voice Hard *kraa.*
Habitat Coasts, lakes, rivers.
Range Locally along all coasts and inland as far north as tundra; very disjointed.
Movements Winters, Gulf Coast, Florida and adjacent Atlantic Coast.

Black Tern

Chlidonias niger

9–10in/23–26cm

Identification Adult in summer is black with slate-gray wings and white undertail. In winter, is white below, slate-gray above with black cap and dark smudge at side of breast. Hawks insects over water.

Voice High-pitched *kik*.

Habitat Marshes, lakes.

Range Breeds right across temperate Canada and throughout northern and western states.

Movements Regular migrant to South America.

Common Murre

Uria aalge 15½–17i/40–44cm

Identification Chunky, short-winged seabird with blackish upperparts washed with dark brown. Bill is pointed. In summer, dark upperparts extend to breast; in winter, only to sides of head. A varying proportion of Atlantic birds have a bridle of white eye-ring and line across cheek.

Voice Growls.

Habitat High-cliffs, winters at sea.

Range Breeds from Labrador to Gulf of St Lawrence in east; and from western Alaska to coast of California in west.

Movements Winters at sea near breeding colonies.

Thick-billed Murre

Uria lomvia 16–18in/41–46cm

Identification Very similar to Common murre, but blacker with thicker bill and pale line along base of upper mandible. In winter, shows darker face than Common Murre.
Voice Growls.
Habitat Cliffs; winters at sea.
Range Overlaps with, but breeds farther north than Common Murre. Abundant among Canadian archipelago, in Alaska and locally in Labrador.
Movements Seldom progresses much farther south than breeding grounds, though may be commonest Murre off east coast of US.

Pigeon Guillemot

Cepphus columba 13½–14in/34–36cm

Identification Very similar to Black Guillemot, but with white patch on wing divided by black wedge. Underwing dark in all plumages. In winter is darker on head and neck.
Voice Whistles.
Habitat Broken cliffs; winters inshore.
Range Breeds from Alaska to California.
Movements Winters near breeding stations.

Horned Puffin

Fratercula corniculata

14–15in/35–38cm

Identification Similar to Common Puffin, but with even larger red and yellow bill. In winter, depth of bill creates a notch between bill and forehead. Horn extending upwards from eye invisible except at extreme close range.
Voice Various *arrs*.
Habitat Crumbling cliffs in summer; at sea in winter.
Range Confined to coasts of Alaska.
Movements Local dispersal, but mostly stays near breeding colonies.

Tufted Puffin

Lunda cirrhata

14–15in/35–38cm

Identification Similar to other puffins, but plumage black above and below. In summer, face is white, long golden tufts extend from the eye and the huge bill is orange-red with a creamy-buff base to the upper mandible. In winter, tufts are lost, whole head is black and bill is slightly reduced.
Voice Growls.
Habitat Sea-cliffs; winters at sea.
Range Pacific Coast from Alaska to California.
Movements Winters offshore at sea.

Rhinoceros Auklet

Cerorhinca monocerata

14–15in/35–38cm

Identification A large, bulky auklet with a chunky bill. Upperparts are blackish; underparts slaty-brown. In summer, there is a 'rhino-like' horn at the base of the yellow bill, plus two tufty plumes on the side of the head. In winter, the horn disappears and the plumes are reduced to two pale lines.
Voice Growls.
Habitat Coastal islands; winters inshore.
Range Breeds from Alaska to southern California.
Movements Large flocks gather along coasts of British Columbia and the Pacific Coast of the US.

Cassin's Auklet

Ptychoramphus aleuticus 8–9in/20–23cm

Identification A dull, sooty auklet marked by short, black bill with a yellow spot at the lower base and a bold, broken white eye-ring. Undertail and belly white.
Voice Repeated croaks.
Habitat Islands; winters at sea.
Range From Alaska to British Columbia.
Movements Often out of sight of land south of breeding range.

Marbled Murrelet

Brachyramphus marmoratus 8½–10in/22–25cm

Identification in summer, marbled brown and chestnut above, brown and buff below, with pale broken eye-ring. In winter, slate-gray above, white below. There is a white patch on the wing (scapulars) and the dark cap extends below the white-rimmed eye. The similar Kittlitz's Murrelet is confined to Alaska, lacks white eye-ring in summer, and has dark cap terminating well above the dark eye in winter.

Voice Repeated *keer* notes.
Habitat Inland screes and trees; winters coasts.
Range Pacific Coast southward to California.
Movements Mainly resident.

Ancient Murrelet

Synthliboramphus antiquus 8½–10in/22–25cm

Identification In summer black head and breast is broken by white crown plumes. The back is gray, separated from the white underparts by a black lateral slash. The small bill is yellow. In winter is similarly, but less boldly, marked. In flight, the black, flank-slash separates white underparts from white wing linings.
Voice Whistles.
Habitat Islands; coasts in winter.
Range Alaska to British Columbia in summer.
Movements Winters from Alaska south to California.

Band-tailed Pigeon

Columba fasciata 14–14½in/35–37cm

Identification Large dark pigeon with purple head and breast, white half collar and iridescent hind neck. In flight, appears uniformly dark, though gray on inner wing and on tail may be useful features.
Voice *Coo-cooo.*
Habitat Conifer and mixed woods, gardens.
Range Breeds Pacific Coast and south-western states.
Movements Winters California.

Rock Dove

Columba livia 11½–12½in/29–32cm

Identification The town pigeon with a wide variety of plumages. Pure wild birds are gray with two black wing bars and white rump.
Voice *Ooo-roo-coo,* repeated.
Habitat Cliffs, cities.
Range Whole of temperate North America.
Movements Resident.

White-winged Dove

Zenaida asiatica 10½–11½in/27–29cm

Identification Dark, olive-green dove with bold white wing patches, obvious both at rest and in flight. White tipped tail shows well.
Voice *Hooo-hooo-hoo-hooo.*
Habitat Dry woods, orchards, semi-desert.
Range Mexican border, locally abundant.
Movements Winters, Mexico and Gulf Coast to Florida.

Mourning Dove

Zenaida macroura

11½–12in/29–31cm

Identification Brown upperparts spotted black; rich pinkish on breast. In flight, appears uniformly dark, but long pointed tail has brown white margins.
Voice *Oooh-oo-oo-oo.*
Habitat Farms, towns, cities.
Range Most widespread pigeon. Breeds throughout US and southern Canada.
Movements Northern birds move southwards to winter.

Scaly-breasted Ground Dove

Columbina passerina 6–7in/16–18cm

Identification Gray-brown above with black spots on folded wings. Male has gray crown and pinkish breast, heavily scaled. Female is grayer. In flight, shows rusty outer wing. *See* Inca Dove.
Voice *Hoo-ah* rising.
Habitat Brush country and open ground.
Range Mexican border country and across Gulf Coast states to Florida.
Movements Resident.

Inca Dove

Columbina inca 7½–8½in/19–22cm

Identification Similar to Scaly-breasted Ground Dove, but heavily marked with scaly crescents above and below. Shows chestnut in wing, particularly in flight, but also has long, rounded tail with black and white margins.
Voice *Coo-coo.*
Habitat Dry semi-desert, often near buildings.
Range Mexican border country.
Movements Resident.

Yellow-billed Cuckoo

Coccyzus americanus

10½–11½in/27–29cm

Identification Slim, long-tailed bird; brown above and white below. Stout, pointed bill has yellow lower mandible, but separated from similar Black-billed Cuckoo by rust in wings, and boldly barred black and white undertail.
Voice Sharp *kuk-kuk-kuk*.
Habitat Woodland, groves.
Range Throughout US, but scarce or absent California and north-west states. Barely penetrates southernmost Canada.
Movements Summer visitor.

Black-billed Cuckoo

Coccyzus erythrophthalmus

10½–11½in/27–29cm

Identification Similar shape, size and coloration as Yellow-billed Cuckoo. Separated by having no rust in wing and only tips of tail feathers marked black and white.
Voice *Co-co-co.*
Habitat Streamside woods.
Range Northern, eastern and central US, together with southern Canada.
Movements Summer visitor.

Greater Roadrunner

Geococcyz californianus 22–23in/56–59cm

Identification Well known, ground-dwelling bird with heavily spotted upperparts, bold crest, large black bill and extremely long, black tail. A great runner.
Voice Pigeon-like cooing.
Habitat Mesquite and semi-desert.
Range South-western US.
Movements Resident.

Screech Owl

Otus asio 8½–9in/21–23cm

Identification Variably colored small owl that is often divided into two distinct species. Yellow eyes, prominent ear tufts, bold white spots across folded wing and black-edged, facial disc are all good features.
Voice Wavering whistles and a trill.
Habitat Woods, parks, suburbs.
Range Throughout US northwards along coast of British Columbia to Alaska.
Movements Resident.

Great Horned Owl

Bubo virginianus 22–23in/53–58cm

Identification Huge, powerful owl, with large rounded wings. Upperparts are mottled and barred brown; underparts streaked and closely barred. Prominent ear tufts, facial disc and yellow eyes.
Voice Deep *hooo-hoo-hoo.*
Habitat Forests, mountains, suburbs, parks.
Range Throughout North America save extreme northern tundra.
Movements Resident.

Long-eared Owl

Asio otus

13½–14½in/34–37cm

Identification Medium-sized owl with heavy streaking above and below and prominent ear tufts, facial disc and yellow-orange eyes. Totally nocturnal. Appears tall and slim when discovered perched.
Voice A low *hoo.*
Habitat Forests and woods.
Range Breeds throughout North America south of the tree line, though absent from southern states.
Movements Many boreal-zone birds migrate south. Winters, throughout US, including areas of south where it does not breed.

Short-eared Owl

Asio flammeus 14–15in/36–39cm

Identification Long-winged, diurnal owl that mostly frequents rough ground and marshes. Buffy and heavily streaked above and below, with clear-cut facial disc and yellow eyes. Glides and hovers in search of prey.
Voice Barking in breeding season.
Habitat Marshes, rough ground, tundra.
Range Breeds throughout Canada and the northern half of the US.
Movements Migrates from Canada to winter over most of the US.

Barn Owl

Tyto alba 13–14in/33–36cm

Identification Ghost-like, white-breasted owl with cinnamon upperparts that often hunts late in the day or in the early morning. Breast color varies from white to pale cinnamon.
Voice Hissing and snoring calls.
Habitation Farmland, suburbs, woodland, parks.
Range Breeds across US, though absent from central northern states.
Movements Largely resident.

Snowy Owl

Nyctea scandiaca

21–26in/51–54cm

Identification Large white owl of tundra. Smaller male is white with variable black spotting on wings and flanks. Female is more heavily spotted and barred all over. Rounded head appears small.
Voice Deep hooting.
Habitat Tundra.
Range Northernmost Alaska and Canada, including archipelago.
Movements Irregular in irruptive movements southward across Canada to northern states.

Barred Owl

Strix varia 20–21½in/51–54cm

Identification Medium-sized owl, heavily barred above and streaked below. Black bordered facial disc with ringed face and dark eyes.
Voice *Oo-oo-ooo-oooo.*
Habitat Conifer and other dense woodlands.
Range Breeds across eastern US and Canada extending north and west to British Columbia; colonising westwards.
Movements Resident.

Spotted Owl

Strix occidentalis

17–18in/43–46cm

Identification Similar to Barred Owl, but brown plumage is boldly spotted white above and especially below. Black-edged, facial disc, ringed face and dark eyes.
Voice Various barking notes.
Habitat Wooded gullies and damp forests.
Range Pacific Coast of US and inland in south-western states.
Movements Resident.

Great Gray Owl

Strix nebulosa

$25\frac{1}{2}$–$27\frac{1}{2}$in/65–70cm

Identification Large gray owl, spotted, barred and streaked black. Huge head with facial disc prominently ringed. Small, yellow eyes. Hunts dawn and dusk.
Voice Deep *who* repeated.
Habitat Boreal and mountain conifer forests.
Range Boreal forests of Canada eastward to Great Lakes, southward in Rockies to northern California.
Movements Mainly resident, but some birds do wander a little southward.

Hawk Owl

Surnia ulula

15–16½in/39–42cm

Identification Long-tailed owl of northern forests that is often seen perched openly on a tree top in daylight. Dark gray, heavily spotted white above; heavily barred black below. White facial disc with yellow eyes, boldly bordered black. Long barred tail.
Voice Falcon-like *ki-ki-ki.*
Habitat Conifer forests.
Range Boreal Canada and Alaska from coast to coast.
Movements Resident.

Burrowing Owl

Athene cunicularia

9–10in/23–25cm

Identification Small, ground-dwelling owl with remarkably long legs. Upperparts brown, spotted white; underparts white, neatly barred brown. Head seems small and rounded with prominent white eyebrows and black chin patch. Often perches openly during day.
Voice Quick *coo-cooo.*
Habitat Dry open grassland.
Range Breeds over western half of US northwards just into Canada.
Movements Migrates southward; winters along Mexican border.

Boreal Owl

Aegolius funereus

9–10in/23–25cm

Identification Small gray owl, spotted white above and streaked brown below. White face, with yellow eyes, boldly bordered to form heart-shaped facial disc.
Voice *Hoo-hoo-hoo* repeated.
Habitat Conifer forests.
Range Boreal Canada to Alaska, also in several areas of Rockies.
Movements Resident.

Northern Saw-whet Owl

Aegolius acadicus 7½–8½in/19–21cm

Identification Small owl with brown upperparts liberally spotted white; underparts white, boldly streaked rust. Facial disc is radially streaked rufous and brown.
Voice Repeated single whistle.
Habitat Dense conifer and mixed forests.
Range Most of US and southern Canada extending northwards to Alaska along Pacific coast. Absent central and southern states.
Movements Some movement to areas of center and south where it does not breed.

Flammulated Owl

Otus flammeolus

6–7in/16–18cm

Identification Small, heavily barred and streaked owl, with nighthawk-type camouflage. Small ear tufts, dark eyes. Appears in rufous and gray phases.
Voice Series of single hoots.
Habitat Extensive woods.
Range Western states coinciding with Rockies.
Movements Summer visitor.

American Pygmy Owl

Glaucidium gnoma

6–7in/16–18cm

Identification Small owl with rounded head, spotted facial disc and yellow eyes. Underparts streaked. Some birds are brown (red phase), some gray (gray phase). Flies fast and direct, often during daylight.
Voice *Hoo-hoo*.
Habitat Woodlands.
Range Breeds in Rocky Mountain system and foothills.
Movements Resident.

Elf Owl

Micrathene whitneyi 5½–6in/14–15cm

Identification Tiny, desert owl, barred and spotted in browns, buffs and chestnut. Rounded head with black bordered facial disc and yellow eyes. Roosts and nests in saguaros; active dawn and dusk.
Voice Repeated chirrups.
Habitat Saguaro deserts and dry woods.
Range Mexican border country.
Movements Summer visitor.

Whip-poor-will

Caprimulgus vociferus
9½–10in/24–26cm

Identification Grayish nightjar, considerably smaller than Chuck-will's-widow. Black chin and white throat-crescent more prominent in male, which has white tail corners in flight.
Voice *Whip-poor-will.*
Habitat Conifer and mixed woods.
Range Breeds most of eastern and south-western US.
Movements Migrates south, but winters in Florida and along Gulf Coast.

Poor-will

Phalaenoptilus nuttallii

7½–8½in/19–21cm

Identification Small nightjar mottled in shades of gray and brown, with white-tipped tail and rounded wings. White throat-crescent contrasts with dark chin and black breast.
Voice *Poor-will.*
Habitat Dry open country.
Range Western half of US.
Movements Summer visitor, resident along Mexican border.

Common Nighthawk

Chordeiles minor

9–10in/23–25cm

Identification Dark, gray nightjar with white chin and closely barred black and white underparts. In flight, wings are long and pointed with bold white patch across the primaries. The tail is distinctly forked, with a narrow white band near the tip. Flies by day and night.
Voice Nasal *peent.*
Habitat Grasslands, woods, towns.
Range Virtually whole of sub-tundra North America.
Movements Summer visitor.

Lesser Nighthawk

Chordeiles acutipennis

8½–9in/21–23cm

Identification Similar to Common Nighthawk, but paler and with less clear-cut barring. Best distinctions are more rounded wings, with white primary patch nearer wing tip; and notched (not forked) tail with broad white band and several smaller bands.
Voice Rapid trilling.
Habitat Dry scrub, semi-desert.
Range Mexican border states.
Movements Summer visitor.

Black Swift

Cypseloides niger 6½–7in/17–18cm

Identification An all-black swift with notched tail; largest of our regular swifts. Breeds among cliffs in west; decidedly scarce.
Voice Repeated *plik-plik*.
Habitat Sheltered cliffs and canyons.
Range From southern Alaska through British Columbia and sporadically through Pacific states.
Movements Summer visitor.

Vaux's Swift

Chaetura vauxi

4½in/11–12cm

Identification Similar to Chimney Swift, but slightly shorter in the wing and paler on breast. Short, square-cut tail.
Voice Soft chattering.
Habitat Nests in hollow trees, sometimes chimneys.
Range Pacific Canada, Alaska and sporadically in western states.
Movements Summer visitor. Note that Chimney Swift and Vaux's Swift can occur together on migration in southern California.

Chimney Swift

Chaetura pelagica 4½–5in/12–13cm

Identification Dark brown above and below, with paler gray, buffy throat and upper breast. Tail short and cut abruptly square. Only swift in the east and could be confused only with Vaux's Swift.
Voice Loud chatter.
Habitat Breeds in chimneys, trees.
Range US and southern Canada east of Rockies.
Movements Summer visitor.

White-throated Swift

Aeronautes saxatalis 6–6½in/16–17cm

Identification Large swift marked by bold black and white pattern above and below. Only swift with white on underparts. Tail distinctly forked.
Voice Shrill chattering.
Habitat Cliffs and canyons.
Range Mountains of the western US.
Movements Migrates, but resident in Mexican border states.

Broad-tailed Hummingbird

Selasphorus platycerus 4in/10cm

Identification Green above, with metallic, ruby-colored throat in male. Thus very similar to Ruby-throated which it replaces in the west. One of best features is that wing beats produce a loud whistle. Female has white throat and pale, rufous wash on flanks.
Voice Hard *chip*.
Habitat Mountain thickets, glades.
Range Rocky Mountains and foothills.
Movements Summer visitor.

Calliope Hummingbird

Stellula calliope 3in/8cm

Identification Tiny hummingbird with green upperparts and white below. Male has ruby throat-streaks; female has spotted throat with pale, rufous wash on flanks.
Voice *See-ree*
Habitat Mountain glades, canyons.
Range Rocky Mountains and foothills.
Movements Summer visitor.

Anna's Hummingbird

Calypte anna 4in/10cm

Identification Metallic green above, whitish below. In male, whole head has a pale, rosy-ruby color; female has rosy speckles on white chin; juvenile has neat black streaking.
Voice A hard *tic*
Habitat Lowland woods and gardens.
Range Pacific coast south to Arizona, north to Vancouver.
Movements Largely resident.

Black-chinned Hummingbird

Archilochus alexandri 4in/10cm

Identification Male has violet throat, becoming black on chin, though in most lights the 'bib' looks totally black. Female very similar to female Ruby-throated.
Voice Quiet *tu*.
Habitat Dry scrub, open woods, suburbs.
Range Western and south-western US.
Movements Summer visitor; some winter in south-eastern states.

Costa's Hummingbird

Calypte costae 3½in/9cm

Identification Tiny hummer with violet head in male extending along sides of neck. Female, green above, white below with all but center feathers of tail gray, tipped black and white.
Voice Penetrating *tink*.
Habitat Dry, arid hillsides and scrub.
Range Southern California and Arizona.
Movements Migrant, but some winter in breeding areas.

Rufous Hummingbird

Selasphorus rufus 4in/10cm

Identification Adult male is reddish on body, with green wings and ruby-colored throat. At all ages, the tail is reddish tipped black. Female is green above with ruby spots on throat. Only Allen's Hummingbird can be confused.
Voice An abrupt *chup*.
Habitat Woodland edges and glades.
Range From southern Alaska southwards through British Columbia to northern California.
Movements Summer visitor.

Allen's Hummingbird

Selasphorus sasin 4in/10cm

Identification Male has green back and crown, ruby throat and rufous underparts and tail. Female not reliably separate from female Rufous Hummingbird.
Voice *Chup*
Habitat Wooded ravines, parks, gardens.
Range Breeds coastal California.
Movements Summer visitor.

Belted Kingfisher

Ceryle alcyon 12½–13½in/32–34cm

Identification The only North American kingfisher. Male has blue-gray upperparts, crown and crest, and breast band. Breast and collar are white. Female differs in having a rich-chestnut breast band. The long bill is gray. This is a great hovering bird that dives to catch fish. Ringed Kingfisher of south-western Texas has underparts chestnut.
Voice Loud rattle.
Habitat Ponds, rivers, lakes, creeks.
Range Breeds throughout sub-tundra North America except south western US.
Movements Northern and central birds are migratory.

Northern Flicker

Colaptes auratus 12–13in/30–33cm

Identification North American flickers were, until recently, regarded as three separate species. Yellow-shafted, Red-shafted and Gilded. All are brown on back and wings spotted with black; white below, similarly spotted black with a black breast-crescent and white rump. Western birds have a red malar stripe; eastern birds a black one. In flight, the underwing is rufous (Red-shafted) or yellow. These are expert climbers that are frequently also seen on the ground.
Voice *Wik-wik-wik.*
Habitatio Woods, suburbs, but also remote areas.
Range From tundra southwards throughout North America, but absent central Texas.
Movements Most Canadian birds move southwards.

Pileated Woodpecker

Dryocopus pileatus 15½–17in/40–43cm

Identification Large, black woodpecker with white facial lines and red crest. Male also has red malar stripe. In flight, underwing has white linings. Confusable only with the presumed extinct Ivory-billed Woodpecker which has white 'V' on back and white secondaries forming a white 'lower back' when perched. In flight, Ivory-bill has broad white trailing edge to wings, both above and below.
Voice *Wucka-wucka-wucka.*
Habitat Forests and parks.
Range Breeds through most eastern states and westwards across southern and central Canada. Also southwards through Pacific states.
Movements Resident.

Gila Woodpecker

Centurus uropygialis 9–10in/23–25cm

Identification Similar to Golden-fronted and Red-bellied Woodpeckers with black and white 'ladder-back'. Male has red on top of crown; female has plain buffy head.
Voice *Churr.*
Habitat Dry scrub, saguaro scrub, towns.
Range Arizona and neighboring California.
Movements Resident.

Ladder-backed Woodpecker

Picoides scalaris 6½–7½in/17–19cm

Identification Typical black and white woodpecker with black and white barred upperparts producing 'ladder-back'. Underparts buffy, spotted black. Male has red crown and distinctive black line across side of head enclosing the 'cheeks'. Female has similar face pattern and black crown.
Voice Sharp *pic.*
Habitat Dry semi-desert, towns.
Range States bordering Mexico.
Movements Resident.

Nuttall's Woodpecker

Picoides nuttallii 7–7½in/18–19cm

Identification 'Ladder-backed' woodpecker similar to that bird, but with ladder not extending to black nape. Male has red hind crown and black cheeks, making it the darkest 'faced' of the group. Female lacks red on crown.
Voice *Week*.
Habitat Wooded canyons.
Range California.
Movements Resident.

Red-headed Woodpecker

Melanerpes erythrocephalus 9–10in/23–25cm

Identification Boldly black, white and red woodpecker. Adult has whole head red, upperparts black, with white rump and white secondaries.
Voice *Querk.*
Habitat Woods, parks, gardens.
Range US and southern Canada east of the Rockies.
Movements Northern and western birds are migrants.

Acorn Woodpecker

Melanerpes formicivorus 8½–9½in/22–24cm

Identification Shiny black above, white below with red crown, black around base of bill and broad, black breast band becoming streaky on belly. Prominent white rump. Stores acorns in holes in bark of trees or telegraph poles.
Voice Harsh *ja-cob.*
Habitat Oak woods, or mixed woods with oaks.
Range California and south-western states.
Movements Resident.

Lewis' Woodpecker

Melanerpes lewis 10–11in/26–28cm

Identification Very dark, metallic-green woodpecker with dark-red face, grayish-pink belly and pale-gray collar, that is particularly obvious in flight. Often catches insects in air; gregarious in winter.
Voice Mostly silent.
Habitat Open woods.
Range Throughout western states northward into British Columbia.
Movements Northern birds migrate southwards.

White-headed Woodpecker

Picoides albolarvatus 9–10in/23–25cm

Identification All-black woodpecker marked by white head, red spot on hind crown and white in outer wing, particularly obvious in flight. Feeds on pine cones.
Voice *Chick*
Habitat Pine forests.
Range Pacific US.
Movements Resident.

Yellow-bellied Sapsucker

Sphyrapicus varius 8½in/21–22cm

Identification Highly variable bird; but with black and white 'ladder-back', white wing coverts and yellowish belly. Head and breast color varies from black, white and red stripes to uniformly red (in the now conspecific Red-breasted Sapsucker). Excavates series of holes in trees to feed on sap and insects attracted by it.
Voice Mostly silent.
Habitat Deciduous and conifer forests.
Range Most of North America except open plains.
Movements Whole population migrates south to winter in southern states and Mexico.

Williamson's Sapsucker

Sphyrapicus thyroideus 8½–9in/22–23cm

Identification Male is mainly black with white lines on face, a red chin, white wing coverts and a yellow belly. Its range overlaps Yellow-bellied Sapsucker. Female has black and white 'ladder-back', brown head and black and white barred underparts. Both sexes have a white rump.
Voice Nasal *cheer*.
Habitat Pine forests.
Range Rocky Mountains from Canadian border to Mexico.
Movements Northern birds migrate.

Hairy Woodpecker

Picoides villosus 9–10in/23–24cm

Identification Medium-sized, pied woodpecker marked by white back and white barring on black wings. Black and white face pattern with red on rear crown of male. *See* Downy Woodpecker.
Voice *Peek.*
Habitat Dense forests.
Range Most sub-tundra areas of North America.
Movements Resident.

Downy Woodpecker

Picoides pubescens 6–6½in/16–17cm

Identification Similarly marked, but much smaller version of Hairy Woodpecker with white back, barred wings and red spot on hind crown of male. Tiny bill is diagnostic.
Voice *Pik.*
Habitat Woods, parks, gardens.
Range Virtually whole of sub-tundra North America.
Movements Resident.

Black-backed Three-toed Woodpecker

Picoides arcticus

9–9½in/23–24cm

Identification Black above, white below, heavily barred black. Face pattern consists of finest of white lines behind eye and bold black zig-zag line across white cheek and neck. Male has golden crown, lacking in female.
Voice Hard *kip*.
Habitat Conifer forests.
Range Boreal Canada southwards through Rockies.
Movements Resident.

Northern Three-toed Woodpecker

Picoides tridactylus 8½in/21–22cm

Identification Similar to Black-backed Three-toed, but has white and black 'ladder-back' (sometimes pure white) and widening white stripe extending behind eye.
Voice *Pik*.
Habitat Conifer forests.
Range Boreal Canada southwards through Rockies.
Movements Resident.

Scissor-tailed Flycatcher

Tyrannus forficatus

12½–13½in/32–34cm

Identification Adult, marked by very long outer tail feathers creating extremely deep forked tail. Head and back dove gray; wings, black with feathers broadly edged white. Underparts, rich pink, extending to underwing linings. Juvenile lacks extreme tail length and pink on underside; wing linings show subdued pink.
Voice *Ka-leep.*
Habitat Farms, scrub, open country.
Range Southern western states, Texas and beyond.
Movements Summer visitor, some winter southernmost Florida.

Vermilion Flycatcher

Pyrocephalus rubinus 5½–6in/14–15cm

Identification Adult male unmistakable with vividly red crown and underparts. Female is buff-brown above with dark ear coverts, streaked breast and a warm, orange-red wash on the belly. Immature male has red belly and a few red feathers on throat and crown. Immature female has yellow wash on belly.
Voice A pleasant *pit-a-see* repeated.
Habitat Aquatic woods and tangles.
Range Mexican border states.
Movements Northernmost birds move to Mexican border.

Eastern Kingbird

Tyrannus tyrannus

8½in/21–22cm

Identification Black crown, dark gray back and wings, with black tail, broadly tipped white. Underparts are dusky white, with subtle gray breast band. Generally perches openly.
Voice *Zeet* repeated.
Habitat Woodland edges, farms, usually near water.
Range Breeds over most of sub-tundra North America, but absent from west and south-west.
Movements Summer visitor.

Western Kingbird

Tyrannus verticalis 8½in/21–22cm

Identification Gray head and breast, yellow belly, olive-gray back combine with black wings and tail, the latter with white outer feathers. This is the widespread tyrant flycatcher of the west and forms a basis from which other 'yellow' flycatchers should be separated with care. Perches openly, upright, with large bill and head prominent. Often appears nervous.
Voice *Whit.*
Habitat Open country with scrub and fences.
Range Common over western US northward into adjacent Canada.
Movements Summer visitor, migrant through eastern US.

Cassin's Kingbird

Tyrannus vociferans 8½–9in/22–23cm

Identification Very similar to Western Kingbird, but buffy tips to tail and lack of white margins are good features. Gray head marked by whiter chin and pale margins to wing feathers are further distinction. Separate with care.
Voice *Chi-hew.*
Habitat Usually denser thickets in dry country than Western Kingbird.
Range From coastal California through adjacent western states northwards to Wyoming.
Movements Summer visitor.

Ash-throated Flycatcher

Myiarchus cinerascens 8½in/21–22cm

Identification Brown upperparts with rust in tail and wing like Great Crested. Pale gray throat and pale yellow underparts are best distinctions. Bill thinner, generally paler than other flycatchers.
Voice Short *ka-wheer.*
Habitat Western woods, scrub, semi-desert.
Range Breeds west of a line drawn from western Texas to Oregon.
Movements Summer visitor, a few winter extreme south-west US.

Eastern Phoebe

Sayornis phoebe 6½–7in/17–18cm

Identification: A rather dull little bird that is brown above and white below, with short, all-black bill. Raises and spreads tail continuously when perched. In fall, a yellow wash covers belly. Pewees have generally larger, pale-based bills.
Voice *Fee-be.*
Habitat Farms, suburbs.
Range Breeds over most of eastern US extending northwards through Canadian prairies and beyond.
Movements Most birds are summer visitors, but winter along Atlantic and Gulf coasts and over much of south-eastern US.

Black Phoebe

Sayornis nigricans 6–6½in/16–17cm

Identification Boldly black and white bird with chunky body and longish tail, which is pumped up and down. Black upperparts, head and breast; white belly and outer tail feathers. Juvenile is browner above with rusty margins to wing coverts.
Voice *Pee-wee.*
Habitat Stream and lake margins; parks in winter.
Range California and south-western US.
Movements Resident over most of range.

Say's Phoebe

Sayornis saya 7–7½in/18–19cm

Identification Buffy brown above, with black tail and rusty belly and undertail coverts. Though rather nondescript, the black tail is wagged and spread like other phoebes.
Voice *Pee-ee.*
Habitat Dry rocky areas, farmsteads.
Range Whole of western North America from Alaska to western Texas and into the prairies.
Movements Summer visitor, though some birds winter in south-western US.

Yellow-billed Flycatcher

Empidonax flaviventris 5–5½in/13–14cm

Identification One of highly confusing group of mainly olive-colored flycatchers marked by bold eye-ring and pale, double wing-bar. Identification often rests on minor plumage features. This species has yellow throat, extensive olive breast, tiny bill with pale lower mandible.
Voice *Per-wee.*
Habitat Northern conifer forests.
Range Boreal Canada and north-eastern US.
Movements Summer visitor; scarce on migration.

Alder Flycatcher

Empidonax alnorum $5\frac{1}{2}$–6in/14–15cm

Identification Darkish flycatcher with medium-strength eye-ring and long, black tail. Very similar to Willow Flycatcher with which previously regarded as conspecific; rather greener above and eye-ring much more obvious.
Voice *Fee-bew.*
Habitat Boggy woods of birch and alder in conifer zone.
Range Boreal Alaska and Canada to north-eastern US.
Movements Summer visitor.

Willow Flycatcher

Empidonax traillii $5\frac{1}{2}$–6in/14–15cm

Identification Dark flycatcher, even darker than closely related Alder Flycatcher, from which it should be separated only with the greatest of care. Lack of eye-ring is best field mark.
Voice *Fitz-beu.*
Habitat Meadows, streamsides, thickets.
Range Right across US, but absent from southern states.
Movements Summer visitor.

Least Flycatcher

Empidonax minimus

4½–5in/12–13cm

Identification Small flycatcher with large-headed appearance, bold eye-ring and dark olive, or olive-brown upperparts. White throat and gray breast are good features; bill appears small with pale base to lower mandible.
Voice *Che-bek.*
Habitat Open woodland, farmland, orchards.
Range From boreal zone southwards into the northern US.
Movements Summer visitor.

Hammond's Flycatcher

Empidonax hammondii 5–5½in/13–14cm

Identification Small, western flycatcher with boldish eye-ring. Appears large headed, with small bill and short tail. Best field mark is gray head contrasting with olive-gray back and breast. Gray-edged tail frequently wagged.
Voice *Peek*
Habitat Mountain conifers.
Range Rocky Mountains from central Alaska southwards to California.
Movements Summer visitor.

Dusky Flycatcher

Empidonax oberholseri

5½–6in/14–15cm

Identification Medium-sized, dully colored flycatcher. Brown above with white throat, olive-gray breast and pale lemon-yellow belly. Bill dark with pale base to lower mandible; tail long, black and narrowly edged white.
Voice *Wit.*
Habitat Bushy mountain slopes.
Range Rocky Mountains, but not as far north as Alaska.
Movements Summer visitor.

Gray Flycatcher

Empidonax wrightii 5½–6in/14–15cm

Identification Pale gray, washed-out flycatcher with pale head, white chin and belly and grayish breast. White eye-ring present, but not obvious on pale gray head. Has the habit of pumping tail downwards.
Voice Loud *whit.*
Habitat High mountain brushland and pines.
Range Rocky Mountains of US.
Movements Summer visitor.

Western Flycatcher

Empidonax difficilis

5–5½in/13–14cm

Identification Olive-brown above with very bold eye-ring, but relatively narrow wing-bars. Chin and belly both yellow separated by extensive olive breast. Tail is long and lower mandible a clear orange.
Voice *Wee-seet* or *sweet.*
Habitat Woods and forests.
Range From Alaskan panhandle through western US.
Movements Summer visitor.

Western Wood Pewee

Contopus sordidulus 6in/15–16cm

Identification Virtually indistinguishable from Eastern Wood Pewee. Lower mandible may be all dark, but also may be orange.
Voice *Peer;* also three note *swee-tee-tee.*
Habitat Deciduous woods.
Range Western North America from Alaska to westernmost Texas.
Movements Summer visitor.

Olive-sided Flycatcher

Contopus borealis

7–7½in/18–19cm

Identification Closely related to the wood pewees. A chunky flycatcher with stout bill and short tail. Upperparts brown with white tufts sometimes visible on inner part of wing. Heavily streaked breast and white throat are best field marks.
Voice A whistled *whip-three beers.*
Habitat Conifer bogs.
Range Boreal zone from Alaska to Newfoundland southwards through the Rockies and Great Lakes.
Movements Summer visitor.

Horned Lark

Eremophila alpestris 7–7½in/17–18cm

Identification Brown and buff streaked above, with black crown patch and horns, black through eye and black breast crescent. Face usually yellow, flanks usually streaked chestnut.
The 'face' pattern is distinctive. Horns often difficult to see.
Voice A high-pitched *seee.*
Habitat Breeds among tundra, bare plains, mountains; winters on bare fields and along shorelines.
Range Breeds over most of Alaska and Canada south throughout most of US.
Movements Canadian birds move mainly into US; winter visitor only in south-east.

Barn Swallow

Hirundo rustica 6–6½in/16–17cm

Identification Metallic blue-black above, rusty below. Long angled wings and deeply forked tail with extended streamers in adult. Chestnut-red face. Nests in rural buildings.
Voice High-pitched chatter.
Habitat Open farmland with buildings.
Range Temperate North America north to tree line.
Movements Summer visitor.

Cliff Swallow

Hirundo pyrrhonota 5–5½in/13–14cm

Identification Similar to Barn Swallow, but browner above with distinct rusty rump; pale grayish below, with reddish face and dark blue-black cap and throat; square tail. Easily separated from all North American swallows except Cave Swallow which is rare in south-west Texas. That bird lacks black throat of Cliff Swallow.
Voice Sweet single call.
Habitat Farms and/or cliffs.
Range Breeds virtually throughout North America except extreme north and south-east, where, however, it is spreading.
Movements Summer visitor.

Violet-green Swallow

Tachycineta thalassina 4½–5in/12–13cm

Identification A 'black and white' swallow that shows an iridescent green on back and inner wing only on a close approach. Similar to Tree Swallow, but with white cheek extending above eye so that it stands out; and white rump divided by black center. Tail is square cut; flight more erratic than Tree Swallow.
Voice A twittering.
Habitat Woods, gardens.
Range Rocky Mountains to western coasts.
Movements Summer visitor, resident central California.

Tree Swallow

Tachycineta bicolor

5½–6in/14–15cm

Identification Dark metallic blue above, white below. Dark upperparts extend below eye; no white on rump. Flaps and glides in flight. Gregarious and widespread.
Voice Twittering.
Habitat Woodlands near water.
Range Breeds over most of Canada and northern US.
Movements Summer visitor; winters along eastern, southern and western coasts; resident California.

Bank Swallow

Riparia riparia 4½–5in/12–13cm

Identification Small, brown swallow with highly fluttering flight. Brown above, whitish below with distinct brown breast band. Tail distinctly notched. Gregarious, forms dense colonies. *See* Rough-winged Swallow.
Voice A nasal, buzzed twitter.
Habitat Sand cliffs.
Range Throughout North America except extreme north and southern US.
Movements Summer visitor.

American Rough-winged Swallow

Stelgidopteryx serripennis 5–5½in/13–14cm

Identification A chunky, longer-winged, less fluttering version of the Bank Martin. Chin, throat and breast are dusky, lacking the well-defined band of the more abundant bird. Less gregarious than that species, not colonial.
Voice A buzzing twitter.
Habitat Cliffs, river banks.
Range Throughout the US and southern Canada.
Movements Summer visitor, resident southern California and Texas Gulf Coast.

Purple Martin

Progne subis 7½–8in/19–20cm

Identification Large, chunky swallow with all-black plumage in metallic purple. Tail has distinct 'V'. Female has gray mottled underparts. Glides on broader wings than other swallows.
Voice Deep twittering.
Habitat Common where multiple nest boxes are available.
Range Widespread in eastern US extending northwards through Canadian prairies. Patchily distributed through Rockies, but widespread along Pacific Coast.
Movements Summer visitor.

Steller's Jay

Cyanocitta stelleri 10½–11½in/27–29cm

Identification Similar to closely-related Blue Jay, but resident in the west. Has similar crest and long tail, but is dark blue throughout with dark, almost black, head. Dark blue underparts separate from all other jays.
Voice *Shack-shack*
Habitat Coastal and mountain forests.
Range Rocky Mountain system from southern Alaska to California.
Movements Resident.

Scrub Jay

Aphelocoma coerulescens 10½–11½in/27–29cm

Identification Blue head, wings and tail are standard features, along with gray underparts. Color of back varies from pale to dark gray; that of chin from gray to white. Large bill and long tail are characteristic, as is a variably prominent breast band.
Voice Rasping *shreep.*
Habitat Suburbs, scrub, woods.
Range Rocky Mountain system of western US, plus Florida.
Movements Resident.

Pinyon Jay

Gymnorhinus cyanocephalus 10–10½in/25–27cm

Identification Rich, pale blue above and below with darker cap and white streaking on throat. Tail shortish and notched. Gregarious.
Voice Loud mewing.
Habitat Pinyon-juniper forests of western mountains.
Range Central Rockies of US.
Movements Resident.

Gray Jay

Perisoreus canadensis 11–12in/28–30cm

Identification Dove gray above, paler gray below. White on head, 'face' and neck variable, but always the distinctive feature. Bill is short and stubby, tail long. Common and gregarious.
Voice *Whee-oo.*
Habitat Boreal Alaska and Canada, southwards through north-eastern US and the Rockies.
Movements Resident.

Black-billed Magpie

Pica pica 18–19in/46–48cm

Identification Large black and white bird with long, wedge-shaped tail and green-blue gloss on wings and tail. Large black bill on strong head; black above broken by white ovals on folded wings; white below.
Voice Laughing and chuckling calls.
Habitat Woodland and brush country.
Range From southern Alaska southwards through prairies and Rockies.
Movements Resident.

Yellow-billed Magpie

Pica nuttalli 15½–16½in/40–42cm

Identification Plumage as Black-billed Magpie, but bill bright yellow and patch of bare yellow skin around the eye.
Voice Chuckles and laughs.
Habitat Foothills and fields.
Range Sacramento Valley, California.
Movements Resident.

Clark's Nutcracker

Nucifraga columbiana 11½–12in/29–31cm

Identification Large, jay-like bird of mountain forests. Dove-gray above and below; black wings with white tipped secondaries and black and white tail. Pointed black bill; flies with crow-like flaps.

Voice Harsh *kra-a-a.*
Habitat Conifer forests in mountains.
Range US Rockies northwards into adjacent Canada.
Movements Resident, with periodic irruptions into semi-desert areas.

Common Raven

Corvus corax 23–24in/58–61cm

Identification Huge crow with heavy head, long and powerful bill and long, wedge-shaped tail that is particularly obvious in flight. Shaggy throat-feathers can be obvious both in flight and when perched.
Voice Deep croaking call.
Habitat Mountains, forests, tundra.
Range Throughout Alaska and Canada, save the prairies, and in western US and along Appalachians.
Movements Resident.

Chihuahuan Raven

Corvus cryptoleucus 19–19½in/48–50cm

Identification Larger than American Crow, but easily confused; slightly wedge-shaped tail, but smaller bill and head than Common Raven. Most easily distinguished by calls. Formerly called White-necked Raven, but the white bases of the neck feathers are usually obscured in the field.
Voice Low croak, higher pitched than Common Raven.
Habitat Arid lands.
Range South-western US.
Movements More northerly birds move southwards in winter.

American Crow

Corvus brachyrhynchos

16–17½in/41–45cm

Identification Large, all-black bird with powerful bill and square-shaped tail in flight. The North-western Crow is sometimes treated as a separate species. *See also* Fish Crow.
Voice Familiar *caw-caw.*
Habitat Very catholic, favoring wide range of habitats.
Range Most of sub-tundra North America. North-western Crow is found in coastal Alaska and British Columbia.
Movements Most Canadian birds move southward in winter.

Black-capped Chickadee

Parus atricapillus 4½–5in/12–13cm

Identification Buff-brown chickadee with black cap and white cheeks. Separate with care from Carolina Chickadee by white margins to flight feathers forming a distinct, pale wing-panel, and ragged lower edge to black bib. Hybridizes where ranges overlap.
Voice *Chick-a-dee-dee-dee.*

Habitat Gardens, woods, forest clearings.
Range Boreal Alaska and Canada extending southwards over northern half of US.
Movements Resident.

Mountain Chickadee

Parus gambeli 4½–5in/12–13cm

Identification Neat, gray chickadee. Whole body is pale gray above and particularly below. Black bib extends to upper breast, while black cap is separated from black eye-stripe by bold white eyebrow. The latter is the best distinguishing feature.
Voice Harsh *chick-adee-adee-adee.*
Habitat Mountain conifer forests.
Range Rocky Mountains.
Movements Resident.

Boreal Chickadee

Parus hudsonicus 5–5½in/13–14cm

Identification Chunky chickadee, marked by chocolate-brown cap, back and flanks; sooty wings and tail; bib black. The overall impression is of a rather scruffy bird.
Voice Nasal *seek-a-da-da.*
Habitat Conifers.
Range Boreal Alaska and Canada.
Movements Resident.

Chestnut-backed Chickadee

Parus rufescens 5in/13cm

Identification The most obvious feature of this small chickadee is the patches of rich chestnut on back, rump and flanks. Rounded head with black cap is washed grayish; cheeks boldly white; underparts white. California birds lack chestnut on flanks.
Voice Rapid *seek-a-dee-dee.*
Habitat Coniferous forests, but also in deciduous woodland.
Range Pacific Coast from Alaska to California.
Movements Resident.

Plain Titmouse

Parus inornatus 6in/15cm

Identification A plain gray titmouse, darker above than below, and virtually devoid of field marks. A small crest extends from the rear crown and there is a patch of white at the base of the bill. Coastal birds are browner.
Voice *Sic-a-dee-dee.*
Habitat Mixed woodland.
Range Western US in southern Rockies.
Movements Resident.

Bridled Titmouse

Parus wollweberi 5in/13cm

Identification A gray titmouse marked by bold gray and black crest, distinctive black and white face pattern and neat little bib.
Voice High *chick-a-dee-dee.*
Habitat Deciduous mountain woodland.
Range Arizona and New Mexico.
Movements Resident.

Verdin

Auriparus flaviceps
4½in/11cm

Identification Tiny, titmouse-like bird with fine, pointed bill. Adult is gray above, whitish below marked by yellow head and throat and a wedge of maroon at the bend of the wing. Juvenile is browner above and lacks the distinguishing features of the adult. It is thus similar to a Bushtit, but has a shorter tail and browner upperparts.
Voice *Chip-chip-chip* repeated.
Habitat Dry scrubland
Range All states bordering Mexico.
Movements Resident.

Common Bushtit

Psaltriparus minimus

4½in/11cm

Identification Tiny, titmouse-like bird that is usually seen in large flocks busily feeding as they pass. Upperparts are gray, underparts slightly paler. The ear coverts have a warm wash of pale brown, the bill is tiny and the tail long. Coastal birds have a pale brown cap and juvenile males in the south-west have black ear coverts and were formerly regarded as a separate species.
Voice Thin, high-pitched notes.
Habitat Dry woodland, chaparral.
Range Rocky Mountains from Vancouver to western Texas.
Movements Resident.

Wrentit

Chamaea fasciata

6–6½in/16–17cm

Identification A small, brown bird with a long tail. Upperparts dull brown, underparts richer brown and streaked; southern birds are a dull buffy below. Bill is short and pale yellow eye is a good feature.
Voice A trilled *pit-pit-pit-r-r-r.*
Habitat Chaparral.
Range Pacific Coast of US.
Movements Resident.

North American Dipper

Cinclus mexicanus 7–8½in/18–22cm

Identification A chunky, all-gray bird that is seldom, if ever, found far from tumbling, rocky streams. Rotund body, thick neck, short, rounded wings and tiny, often 'cocked' tail are best field marks. White eye-ring and stout yellow legs confirm. Perches on rocks, swims and wades in water.
Voice Loud song and characteristic *zeet* call.
Habitat Fast streams with boulders, long stony glides, weirs, etc.
Range Resident in western Alaska, Canada and US, in Rocky Mountain chain.
Movements Some local movement, especially where streams ice-up in winter.

White-breasted Nuthatch

Sitta carolinensis 5–6in/13–15cm

Identification Boldly-pied bird that climbs up and down trees with equal ease. Crown and nape are black, the remaining upperparts gray with black in wings and white corners to the tail. Underparts white with black eye standing out in contrast.
Voice A repeated nasal whistle *wee-wee-wee,* also a single *hank.*
Habitat Conifer, oak, juniper and other woodlands.
Range Resident US except where forests or woods absent. Just penetrates southern Canada.
Movements Resident in native woodland.

Red-breasted Nuthatch

Sitta canadensis 4½in/11–12cm

Identification: Equivalent of White-breasted Nuthatch in conifer forests, though the two do overlap. Smaller with black cap broken by bold white eyebrow and black stripe running through eye. Gray back, with black and white tail. Underparts a warm rust. Stripe through eye is best field mark.
Voice Nasal *hank-hank-hank*
Habitat Conifer forests in north and in mountains of east and west.
Range Breeds from north-western Canada to California, through the Rockies and in narrow band across the border and Great Lakes region. Also southwards from Newfoundland to the Appalachians.
Movements Irregular movements southwards across US when food crops crash.

Pygmy Nuthatch

Sitta pygmaea 4½in/11cm

Identification The western equivalent of the Brown-headed Nuthatch. Upperparts are blue-gray, underparts creamy-buff. Crown is sooty-black, the cheeks white. A white nape patch can be seen only at close range.
Voice Squeaking calls.
Habitat Ponderosa pines.
Range Patchily distributed through the Rockies and foothills.
Movements Resident.

Brown Creeper

Certhia familiaris 5–6in/13–15cm

Identification Easily overlooked, brown and buff streaked bird, that climbs trunks and major limbs of trees. White underparts, long decurved bill and sharp-pointed tail-feathers are all good marks.
Voice High-pitched *see-see-see.* Attention is usually attracted by call than by a sighting.
Habitat All kinds of woodland and forest.
Range Breeds right across North America in conifer zone and southwards through Rockies and Appalachians.
Movements Winters throughout most of US as far as Gulf Coast.

House Wren

Troglodytes aedon

4½-5in/11-13cm

Identification: A widespread and common small wren. Chunky shape and short 'cocked' tail are characteristic. Upperparts only faintly barred and underparts paler than similar wrens. Generally grayer with no prominent facial marking.
Voice: A loud rising trill, plus various scolding notes.
Habitat: Broad-leaved woods, thickets,often alongside water.
Range: Breeds across US extending northwards into southern Canada.
Movements: Whole population moves southwards to winter along Gulf Coast, southwards to Mexico.

Winter Wren

Troglodytes troglodytes 4in/10cm

Identification Tiny, brown bird very similar to House Wren. Upperparts barred brown, buff and black; underparts brown, heavily barred on belly. Very short tail often held cocked over back. House Wren has longer tail and lacks barring on belly.
Voice Rich explosive warble.
Habitat Conifer woods with dense scrub.
Range Boreal Canada extending northwards into Alaska and southwards along Pacific Coast and the Appalachians.
Movements Canadian birds migrate southwards to winter in southern and eastern states.

Bewick's Wren

Thryomanes bewickii 4½–5in/12–13cm

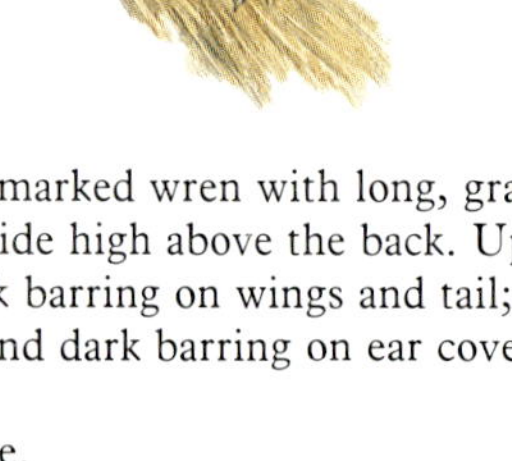

Identification Well-marked wren with long, graduated tail, that is wagged from side to side high above the back. Upperparts brown or gray-brown with black barring on wings and tail; underparts white. Bold white eyebrow and dark barring on ear coverts. Bill, long and decurved.
Voice Buzzing warble.
Habitat Thickets, scrub, woodland clearings.
Range Breeds across southern US, but declining in the east.
Movements Largely resident, but eastern birds move southwards to winter along Gulf Coast.

Cactus Wren

Campylorhynchus brunneicapillus

8–8½in/20–22cm

Identification Large wren of arid landscapes. Heavily barred and streaked in white, black and dark brown above; white on breast and creamy buff on belly, both heavily streaked black. Bold, white eyebrow; long, decurved bill. Tail often cocked.
Voice Harsh *cha-cha-cha*.
Habitat Cactus country, dry hillsides.
Range States adjacent to Mexican border.
Movements Resident.

Rock Wren

Salpinctes obsoletus 5½–6in/14–15cm

Identification Crown, back and wings are gray, spotted white; rump and tail brown, and similarly spotted. Underparts whitish becoming creamy on belly; slight streaking. Short, pale eyebrow.
Voice *Tic-ear* and trilling.
Habitat Rocky gullies, hillsides.
Range Whole of western US and adjacent Canada.
Movements: Northern interior populations are migratory.

Canyon Wren

Catherpes mexicanus 5½–6in/14–15cm

Identification Easily identified by rufous body contrasting with gray crown and white face, throat and breast. But often difficult to see.
Voice Loud rich warble that stutters to a conclusion.
Habitat Dark canyons and gullies.
Range Rocky Mountains and foothills from Canadian border to central Texas.
Movements Some high-level breeders descend in winter.

Marsh Wren

Cistothorus palustris 5in/13cm

Identification Rich, rusty wren found in association with wetlands. Upperparts, rufous heavily barred black with series of bold white stripes on back. Crown, black-brown with lengthy, white eyebrow. Throat and upper breast, white. Formerly known as Long-billed Marsh Wren.
Voice Low *suk*.
Habitat Reed swamps.
Range Right across North America on both sides of Canadian border, locally in southern half of US.
Movements Mostly a summer visitor; winters in southern and coastal states.

Northern Mockingbird

Mimus polyglottos 9–10in/23–25cm

Identification Dove-gray crown, back and rump; contrasting black wings and tail, both showing bold areas of white in flight and display. Underparts, pale gray. Bill, slightly decurved. Readily associates with suburban man.
Voice Accomplished mimic of other birds and natural and unnatural sounds.
Habitat Suburbs, thickets, open woodland.
Range Breeds across southern half of US and northwards along east coast.
Movements Northern interior birds move southward in winter.

Gray Catbird

Dumetella carolinensis 8½in/21–22cm

Identification Uniformly slate-gray bird with black cap and black tail that is often held cocked over back. Rich maroon undertail coverts.
Voice Cat-like *me-ou*.
Habitat Dense cover in woods and suburbs.
Range Breeds across southern Canada and much of US, though absent from south-western quarter of the country and the Gulf Coast.
Movements: Migratory, winters Florida and Gulf Coast and along Atlantic Coast.

Brown Thrasher

Toxostoma rufum

10½–11½in/27–29cm

Identification Rich, rufous brown above with bold cream and black, double wing-bar. Tail long and rounded; bill decurved; eye yellow. Underparts cream, heavily streaked black. Common bird of woods and hedges.

Voice Phrases repeated two or three times.

Habitat Woodland edges, suburbs, hedgerows.

Range Breeds throughout eastern US as far west as the Rockies and northward into adjacent Canada.

Movements Winters in southern and Atlantic states.

Sage Thrasher

Oreoscoptes montanus 8½in/21–22cm

Identification A gray-brown thrasher heavily streaked below. Pale eyes; white, double wing-bar and pale tip to tail are all good field marks.

Voice Extended warbling with no mimicry.

Habitat Sage brush country, semi-desert.

Range Rocky Mountains and foothills in US.

Movements Migratory southward to winter in Mexico and bordering US states.

Bendire's Thrasher

Toxostoma bendirei

9–10in/23–25cm

Identification Gray above; dirty buff below, spotted dark gray. Similar to Curve-billed Thrasher, but bill significantly shorter, with pale base to lower mandible. To be identified with care.
Voice Warbled song, repeated notes.
Habitat Brush country, arid farmland.
Range South-western states.
Movements Most leave the US in winter.

Curve-billed Thrasher

Toxostoma curvirostre 10–11in/26–28cm

Identification Large, gray thrasher with long uniformly dark, decurved bill (*see also* Bendire's Thrasher). Gray upperparts with double, white wing-bar; underparts heavily mottled, or virtually uniformly gray – never delicately streaked like Bendire's.
Voice Pleasant, variable warbling.
Habitat Hillsides, bushlands.
Range South-western US.
Movements Resident.

California Thrasher

Toxostoma redivivum 11½–12in/29–31cm

Identification Large, dark thrasher, with long, heavily decurved black bill. Earth-brown above with pale eyebrow and clear moustachial streak; underparts brown, warmer on belly. Tail long and graduated.
Voice *Chuck*.
Habitat Brushland, chaparral.
Range California.
Movements Resident.

Le Conte's Thrasher

Toxostoma lecontei 10½–11in/27–28cm

Identification Uniform dove-gray thrasher of desert areas that spends most of its time on the ground. Gray body with white chin and fine black moustachial streak; tail black; undertail a warm rufous. Bill is long, black and decurved.

Voice *Tu-eep* call, melodic warbling song.
Habitat Open semi-desert.
Range Southern California and adjacent states.
Movements Resident.

Crissal Thrasher

Toxostoma dorsale

10½–11½in/27–29cm

Identification Dark gray thrasher with long, decurved bill. Upperparts dark gray, paler on rump and crown. White throat accentuates bold, black, moustachial streak. Underparts pale brown. Undertail coverts are rich chestnut. A secretive bird of dense low cover.

Voice Pleasant slow warble, whistling *tu-rip*.

Habitat Dense low vegetation in arid areas.

Range US states bordering Mexico.

Movements Resident.

American Robin

Turdus migratorius 9½–10in/24–25cm

Identification Well-known, common bird marked by brown upperparts and rich-red underparts. Other field marks include boldly broken, white eye-ring, streaked white bib and white tips to the outer tail feathers. Juvenile shows same basic pattern, but is heavily spotted above and below.

Voice Melodic, three-note warble, repeated.

Habitat Suburbs, parks, woodland.

Range Breeds throughout North America.

Movements Canadian and north central US birds are migratory.

Varied Thrush

Ixoreus naevius 9–9½in/23–24cm

Identification A dark thrush with blue of back extending to nape and tail; underparts rich, rust-red with bold, black breast-band. Black wings with bold, rust-red, double wing-bar. Female has earth-brown, not blue, upperparts, but is similarly patterned with rust-red eyebrow being more prominent.
Voice A slow and variable trill.
Habitat Conifer and other forests.
Range From Alaska along Pacific Coast as far as northern California.
Movements Northern birds move southwards as far as southern California in winter.

Townsend's Solitaire

Myadestes townsendi
8½–9in/21–23cm

Identification: A slender gray bird marked by short bill and pale eye-ring. Orange in wing, and white outer feathers of long tail are particularly obvious in flight. Perches openly, sometimes catching insects in the air. Juvenile is brown, spotted and barred above and below.
Voice: Pleasant warble.
Habitat: Mountain conifer forests.
Range: Rocky Mountains from Alaska to Mexican border.
Movements: Alaskan and Canadian birds move southward to winter.

Hermit Thrush

Catharus guttatus 6–6½in/16–17cm

Identification Small thrush with brown upperparts and rust-red tail. Underparts white with large splodges of brown and gray, particularly on the breast. Pale, narrow eye-ring. Colors vary somewhat across North America, but the rufous tail is virtually a constant feature. *See* other small thrushes and Veery.
Voice Fluty warble.
Habitat Woodlands, scrub.
Range Breeds through the boreal zone southwards through the Rockies.
Movements Most birds are migratory, though resident along the Pacific Coast throughout the year. Winters along the Atlantic and in southern US.

Swainson's Thrush

Catharus ustulatus 6½–7in/17–18cm

Identification Earth-brown above with bold eye-ring and pale lores; underparts are warm buff on breast, heavily-spotted with brown; belly whitish, flanks brown-gray. Western form is a warmer shade of brown.
Voice Rising series of whistles.
Habitat Wet scrub, thickets, damp woods.
Range Boreal and Rocky Mountain zones.
Movements Summer visitor.

Gray-cheeked Thrush

Catharus minimus 6½–7in/17–18cm

Identification Small, earth-brown thrush; white underparts clearly spotted brown on the breast, and with a grayish wash along the flanks. Uniform lores and ear coverts, together with insignificant eye-ring, give this bird a somewhat featureless 'face'.
Voice Nasal, Veery-like song.
Habitat Conifer forests, also mixed woodland.
Range Northern taiga zone from Alaska to Newfoundland.
Movements Summer visitor.

Veery

Catharus fuscescens

6½–7in/17–18cm

Identification Warm rufous-brown above, with warm buff on throat and upper breast, delicately streaked; white below with grayish wash on flanks. Pale lores, and ear coverts speckled. Rufous upperparts separate from all other thrushes except Pacific form of Swainson's Thrush.
Voice Series of fluty notes on a descending scale.
Habitat Damp woodlands and riverside thickets.
Range Breeds across the continent either side of the US-Canada border, southwards through the Rockies and Appalachians.
Movements Summer visitor.

Western Bluebird

Sialia mexicana

6½–7in/17–18cm

Identification Structure and behavior as Eastern Bluebird, but male darker, purple-blue above and dark rust below; belly gray rather than white. Female similar to female Eastern, but darker rust on breast.
Voice A repeated *few*.
Habitat Woods, farms, orchards.
Range Western US as far north as British Columbia.
Movements Northern birds migrate, but resident near Pacific Coast.

Mountain Bluebird

Sialia currucoides 6½–7in/17–18cm

Identification Male is blue above, with deep blue wings and tail; underparts pale blue becoming grayish on belly. Female is gray above and below, with blue in wings and tail. Plain featureless 'face' lacks eye-ring of other female bluebirds.
Voice A warbling *tu-lee*.
Habitat High level grasslands.
Range Western US as far north as Alaskan panhandle.
Movements Northern and interior birds migrate southward to Mexican border and beyond.

Blue-gray Gnatcatcher

Polioptila caerulea 4½in/11cm

Identification Small, long-tailed, active and conspicuous bird. Male is bluish-gray above with white eye-ring, black eyebrow, black wings, and long, black, white-edged tail. The underparts are pale gray.
Voice Nasal *wee.*
Habitat Woods, scrub.
Range Breeds across most of US, though absent from north-central and north-western states.
Movements Summer visitor, but resident along Atlantic and Gulf coasts and along Mexican border.

Black-tailed Gnatcatcher

Polioptila melanura 4½in/11cm

Identification Gray above with black cap, blackish wings and black tail with white margins. Female lacks black cap, but has much less white in tail than the Blue-gray Gnatcatcher.
Voice Repeated *gee.*
Habitat Arid brush country, sagebrush, etc.
Range US along Mexican border.
Movements Resident.

Golden-crowned Kinglet

Regulus satrapa 4in/10cm

Identification Tiny, ever-active bird, greenish above, with black wings marked by double, white wing-bar, and black tail. Male has complex 'face' pattern of black eyestripe, white eyebrow and vivid orange-red crest. Female is similar, but with yellow crest.
Voice Thin *see-see-see.*
Habitat Conifer woods.
Range Boreal Canada together with Rockies, Appalachians and northern US.
Movements Northern birds migrate to winter throughout US.

Ruby-crowned Kinglet

Regulus calendula 4½in/11cm

Identification: Similar to Golden-crowned Kinglet with greenish upperparts and black wings with double, white wing-bar. Both sexes show plain face, lacking the distinctive stripes of the Golden-crowned. Male has red crest, but this is seldom a prominent field mark.
Voice: Thin *see-see-see.*
Habitat: Conifer woods and thickets.
Range: Boreal Canada extending southwards through the US Rockies.
Movements: Migratory, wintering southern, western and eastern US.

Buff-bellied Pipit

Anthus rubescens

6–6½in/16–17cm

Identification Previously known as Water Pipit and as American Pipit. A slim, long-tailed bird, brown-gray above, lightly streaked; buffy below with fine streaking on the breast; much heavier streaking in winter. White, outer tail feathers. Spends much time walking; dark legs.
Voice Thin *pee-eet*.
Habitat Tundra, mountains.
Range Northernmost Canada extending southwards through highest Rockies.
Movements Winters south to most areas of US, except the interior.

Sprague's Pipit

Anthus spragueii 6–6½in/16–17cm

Identification Similar to Buff-bellied Pipit, but with pale margins to feathers of upperparts producing a 'scalloped' effect. Dark eye with no obvious stripes; streaking on breast clear-cut; belly white. More white on outer tail than Buff-bellied; pink not dark legs.
Voice Loud *squeet*.
Habitat Grasslands.
Range Canadian and US prairies.
Movements Summer visitor; winters Texas and adjacent states and into Mexico.

Bohemian Waxwing

Bombycilla garrulus 8–8½in/20–21cm

Identification Chubby, olive-brown bird with bold crest, dark 'face' pattern and black wings, with white bar. Tail is shortish and tipped yellow. Waxy marks on wings seldom obvious. *See* Cedar Waxwing.
Voice Buzzy notes.
Habitat Conifer woods.
Range Alaska and western Canada.
Movements Regularly winters north-western US, but irrupts eastwards every few years to areas where it is otherwise unknown.

Cedar Waxwing

Bombycilla cedrorum 6½–7in/17–18cm

Identification Smaller, browner version of Bohemian Waxwing, with similar crest and cross 'face' pattern. Gray rump, white undertail and yellow belly are best means of distinction. Large flocks in winter.
Voice Quiet trilling.
Habitat Conifer and mixed woods.
Range Breeds right across temperate North America in a belt either side of the US-Canada border.
Movements Northern birds regularly migrate over whole of US.

Plainopepla

Plainopepla nitens 7–8in/18–20cm

Identification Male is all-black 'flycatcher' with deep-red eye. A sharp, ragged crest and long, boat-shaped tail are best features, though in the air the primaries show boldly-white centers. Female is uniformly gray, with darker wings and tail.
Voice Whistling *werp*.
Habitat Arid brush.
Range Mexican border states.
Movements Some birds winter along the border.

Northern Shrike

Lanius excubitor 9–10in/23–25cm

Identification Medium-sized gray bird of predatory habits. Crown and back, pale gray with black wings and tail, white rump and black facial mask. Underparts lightly barred; bill large and hooked. Perches openly. In flight, shows bold-white wing flash. *See* Loggerhead Shrike.
Voice Harsh *chack-chack*.
Habitat Open scrub north of boreal zone.
Range Sub-tundra zone of Canada.
Movements Resident south Alaska otherwise moves southward to winter across temperate Canada and US.

Loggerhead Shrike

Lanius ludovicianus

8½–9in/21–23cm

Identification Very similar to slightly larger Northern Shrike. Smaller bill; larger black mask extends above eye and over base of upper mandible; smaller, white wing-patch; and darker shade of gray are the main features to look for.
Voice Harsh *chack-chack*.
Habitat Brush covered areas of scrub.
Range Breeds throughout US northwards into temperate Canada.
Movements Canadian and birds of central northern states move southwards to winter.

Starling

Sturnus vulgaris 8½in/21–22cm

Identification Introduced from Europe and now widespread. Iridescent green and purple sheen on back in summer; heavily spotted white and buff in winter. Short-tail, pointed wings and yellow bill characteristic at all times. Gregarious and aggressive.
Voice Wheezes and mimicry.
Habitat Cities, villages, farmsteads, woods.
Range Temperate and boreal North America.
Movements Some movements, but found throughout breeding range in winter.

Gray Vireo

Vireo vicinior

5–5½in/13–14cm

Identification Gray above with double wing-bar, but only a rudimentary eye-ring. Underparts white, grayish wash on breast. Only the Rocky Mountain form of the Solitary Vireo is all-gray, but this bird has a prominent eye-ring. Chunky vireo-type bill.
Voice Pleasant warbling *chu-eet*
Habitat Dry bush country among rocky cliffs.
Range South-western US.
Movements Summer visitor; winters southern Arizona.

Solitary Vireo

Vireo solitarius 5–5½in/13–14cm

Identification: Widespread, but variable vireo. Eastern birds have gray heads, green upperparts and yellow-streaked flanks. Birds in the Rockies are gray; those on the West coast have olive-green heads. All have bold 'spectacles', double wing-bars and streaked (not washed) flanks.
Voice: Melodic *chu-eet, cheereo, chuwee.*
Habitat: Deciduous and mixed woods.
Range: From boreal zone southwards through the Rockies and through the Great Lakes and Appalachians.
Movements: Winters Florida and Gulf Coast.

Bell's Vireo

Vireo bellii 4½in/12cm

Identification: Olive-gray vireo, with white, double wing-bar and bold eye-ring. Variable plumage, some have indistinct eye-ring and only one faint wing-bar.
Voice Rapid warble of harsh notes.
Habitat Woodland and scrub.
Range South-western and central US.
Movements Summer visitor.

Hutton's Vireo

Vireo huttoni 5in/13cm

Identification Dark olive-gray above, whitish below with yellow wash over flanks. White eye-ring, loral spot and double wing-bar. The eye-ring is broken at the top – a good field mark if approached within close enough range.
Voice Repeated *chee-eet*.
Habitat Damp woods.
Range Pacific Coast and Mexican border states.
Movements Resident.

Red-eyed Vireo

Vireo olivaceus

5½–6in/14–15cm

Identification Olive-brown upperparts marked by gray crown, black lateral coronal stripe, white supercilium and black eye stripe. Only Black-whiskered Vireo of coastal Florida can be confused. Red eye may be difficult to see in field. Yellow sub-species occurs in Texas.
Voice Variable song produced at great length.
Habitat Woods.
Range Eastern US extending northwards through the boreal zone of Canada.
Movements Summer visitor.

Warbling Vireo

Vireo gilvus 5–5½in/13–14cm

Identification Grayish vireo with washed-out, pale foreparts. Back is olive-gray, underparts white; bold supercilium and clear-gray eye-stripe. Lacks wing-bars like Red-eyed and Philadelphia Vireo.
Voice Pleasant warbling.
Habitat Deciduous woodland.
Range Most of vegetated North America, though absent from much of Texas.
Movements Summer visitor.

Black-and-white Warbler

Mniotilta varia 5–5½in/13–14cm

Identification Breeding male is boldly black and white, marked by black chin and ear coverts and much streaking on breast and flanks. Female lacks black chin and has gray ear coverts. In all plumages the striped crown is the best field mark. Climbs tree trunks and branches like a nuthatch.
Voice Thin *wee-see*, repeated.
Habitat Woodlands.
Range Summer visitor to eastern North America extending northwards through western Canada.
Movements Winters Florida and Gulf Coast.

Tennessee Warbler

Vermivora peregrina 4½–5in/12–13cm

Identification Summer male has olive-green upperparts, white underparts and gray crown. Female lacks gray crown and has yellow wash on breast. Non-breeding birds are greener above and below with clear supercilium, single wing-bar and white undertail coverts.
Voice Repeated *seet* on descending scale.
Habitat Deciduous and mixed woodland, feeds in canopy.
Range Boreal zone of Canada and Alaskan panhandle extending across US border in east.
Movements Summer visitor; winters Mexico to northern South America.

Orange-crowned Warbler

Vermivora celata 5–5½in/13–14cm

Identification Dull, greeny-yellow warbler marked by lightly streaked underparts. The orange patch on the crown is seldom visible. Color varies from bright yellowish western birds, to dull olive eastern ones. Immatures are generally greener, like young Tennessee Warblers, but lack white undertail coverts of that bird.
Voice A repeated trill.
Habitat Thickets, open woodland, forest margins.
Range From Alaska through the boreal zone to Labrador and southwards throughout the Rockies.
Movements Winters mainly in Florida and along the Gulf Coast, but also along Atlantic and Pacific coasts.

Nashville Warbler

Vermivora ruficapilla 4½–5in/12–13cm

Identification Dark upperparts and yellow underparts. Female has darker, brownish head and lacks yellow on throat. Fall birds are duller still, with eye ring the only prominent feature.
Voice *See-weet*, high-pitched and repeated, followed by a trill.
Habitat Regenerating woods and damp spruce woodland.
Range Breeds north and south of the Canada-US border in eastern and western populations separated by a gap through the prairies.
Movements Summer visitor; winters southern, coastal California and south-west coast of Texas.

Virginia's Warbler

Vermivora virginiae 4½–5in/12–13cm

Identification Male in summer has gray head and upperparts, with paler gray chin, a yellow breast-patch and yellow under and upper tail coverts. The belly is a dingy white. Bold, white eye-ring. Female is brown-gray with less yellow.
Voice An accelerating series of notes.
Habitat Scrub and thickets at altitude.
Range Southern Rocky Mountain states.
Movements Summer visitor.

Lucy's Warbler

Vermivora luciae 4½in/11cm

Identification Gray above, paler below, with rusty rump and chestnut crown patch. Female has paler rusty areas and immature female may lack rust on crown completely.
Voice A pleasant trill terminating with a series of clear, whistled notes.
Habitat Mesquite scrub, often along dry river beds.
Range South-western US as far as southern California.
Movements Summer visitor.

Northern Parula

Parula americana 4½in/11cm

Indentification A small warbler with blue-gray upperparts marked by a bold, broken eye-ring and bold, double, white wing-bar. The male has a yellow breast, divided by a black and rust breast band; a white belly with a hint of chestnut along the flanks. The female is duller, with no breast band. Fall birds are identified by a combination of wing-bars, broken eye-ring and yellow underparts.
Voice A trill terminating with a single *zit*.
Habitat Conifer and mixed woods, often near swamps.
Range Eastern US and Canada.
Movements Summer visitor; winters southern Florida.

Yellow Warbler

Dendroica petechia 5–5½in/13–14cm

Identification Male is yellow above and below, liberally streaked chestnut on the breast. Female is paler and greener, without streaking. Fall birds are similar to female and best identified by pale spots in the spread tail.
Voice Six or seven *sweet* notes.
Habitat Damp thickets of willow as well as gardens.
Range Virtually throughout North America south of the tundra, but absent much of Texas and Gulf Coast.
Movements Summer visitor; winters southern California.

Magnolia Warbler

Dendroica magnolia 5–5½in/13–14cm

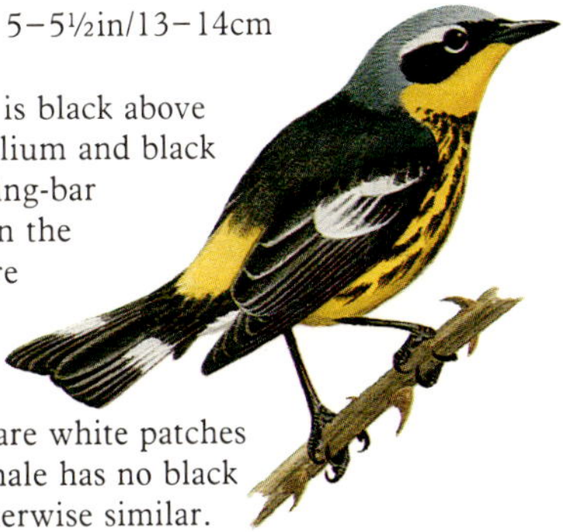

Identification Breeding male is black above with gray crown, white supercilium and black mask. A bold, white, double wing-bar merges to form a broad patch in the closed wing. The underparts are yellow, streaked black, the streaks merging to form a black band across the breast. The rump is yellow and there are white patches at the sides of the tail. The female has no black mask or breast band, but is otherwise similar. Fall birds have a gray crown, grayish breast band, pale supercilium, double wing-bar and yellow rump.

Voice Musical warble.

Habitat Conifer woods.

Range Boreal North America, southwards through Appalachians.

Movements Summer visitor.

Cape May Warbler

Dendroica tigrina 5–5½in/13–14cm

Identification A dark, heavily-streaked warbler. Summer male is olive, streaked black, above; yellow, streaked black, below. Best field marks are white wing patch and yellow 'face' with chestnut ear coverts. Female is similar, but has narrow, double wing-bar and only an orange wash on the 'face'. Fall birds are paler versions, though male retains white wing patch. Yellow rump in all plumages.

Voice High pitched *see-see-see.*

Habitat Spruce forests.

Range Boreal Canada.

Movements Summer visitor.

Yellow-rumped Warbler

Dendroica coronata 5½–6in/14–15cm

Identification Formerly divided into Myrtle and Audubon's Warblers. Basically gray above, streaked black; white below with black breast band and flank streaks. Males have yellow on crown, sides of breast and (in some populations) on throat. Double, white wing-bar, often nearly forming a white wing panel. Female and fall birds are brownish with pale supercilium and streaked breast. Yellow rump in all plumages.
Voice Pleasant warbling.
Habitat Woodland.
Range Widespread in northern and western North America.
Movements Winters over much of southern, eastern and western US.

Townsend's Warbler

Dendroica townsendi 5–5½in/13–14cm

Identification Olive-gray above with bold, double wing-bar; yellow below, streaked black; but with white belly. Distinctive 'face' pattern of dark crown, ear coverts and bib against a background of yellow. Female has yellow, not black, bib.
Voice Buzzing with clear notes to end.
Habitat Conifers.
Range From Alaska to Oregon and into the Rockies.
Movements Winters coastal California.

Black-throated Green Warbler

Dendroica virens 5–5½in/13–14cm

Identification Dark olive above and with black wings marked by double, white wing-bar. Underparts white with black breast band and flank streaks. Male has black throat joining breast band; female has yellowish throat.
Voice Wheezing *zee-zee-zee*.
Habitat Conifer and mixed woods.
Range Boreal Canada, north-eastern US extending southwards through Appalachians.
Movements Summer visitor.

Hermit Warbler

Dendroica occidentalis 5½–6in/14–15cm

Identification Slaty-gray upperparts with double, white wing-bar; whitish below. Both sexes have yellow head and black bib. Female duller than male.
Voice Pleasant warble.
Habitat Conifers.
Range Pacific US.
Movements Winters coastal California.

Black-throated Gray Warbler

Dendroica nigrescens 5–5½in/13–14cm

Identification Male is gray above, lightly streaked black; the underparts are white with black streaking on the flanks. Whole of head, throat and breast are black with bold white supercilium and moustachial streak. Female is slate gray rather than black on head.
Voice Wheezing song.
Habitat Dry woods and scrub.
Range Much of western US to southern British Columbia.
Movements Summer visitor, resident southernmost California.

Grace's Warbler

Dendroica graciae 5–5½in/13–14cm

Identification Very similar to Yellow-throated Warbler, but with yellow supercilium and no white patch behind ear coverts. The overall effect is to make this a darker bird than the Yellow-throated.
Voice Pleasant chipping on same note.
Habitat Conifers, especially yellow pines, and mixed woods.
Range South-western US.
Movements Summer visitor.

Blackpoll Warbler

Dendroica striata 5½–6in/14–15cm

Identification Similar to Black-and-white Warbler, but cap completely black, lacking coronal stripe. Male streaked gray and black above with double, white wing-bar, white cheeks and white underparts heavily streaked black. Female and fall birds are yellowish on head and breast, heavily streaked.
Voice High-pitched *see-see-see.*
Habitat Coniferous woods.
Range Boreal Canada and north-eastern US.
Movements Summer visitor.

Northern Waterthrush

Seiurus noveboracensis 6in/15–16cm

Identification Similar to Louisana Waterthrush, but with smaller bill, lack of buff on flanks and, in particular, shorter and tapering pale supercilium.
Voice Series of loud notes terminating in a slur.
Habitat Damp woods, thickets.
Range Boreal Canada southwards through the Great Lakes and north-eastern US.
Movements Summer visitor; a few winter southern Florida.

Common Yellowthroat

Geothlypis trichas 5–5½in/13–14cm

Identification Olive above and yellow below, marked in the male by bold, black facial mask. Bright red legs. Female lacks mask. Geographical variation affects mostly the amount of yellow on underparts; western birds being brighter than eastern ones.
Voice Repeated *witchy.*
Habitat Overgrown grasslands, thickets.
Range Whole of sub-tundra North America.
Movements Summer visitor, winters southern and coastal states.

Yellow-breasted Chat

Icteria virens 7½–8in/19–20cm

Identification Large, heavy, thickset warbler. Brown above, yellow below. Short, chunky bill with white loral stripe extending to white eye-ring; short white moustachial streak. Generally self-effacing.
Voice Chattering.
Habitat Thickets and scrub.
Range Whole of US except Great Lakes and Florida.
Movements Summer visitor.

MacGillivray's Warbler

Oporornis tolmiei 5–5½in/13–14cm

Identification Upperparts olive-green without wing-bars. Head, gray with broken, white eye-ring; breast gray, with black speckling in male. Underparts entirely yellow; legs red; bill short. *See* Mourning and Connecticut Warblers.
Voice Buzzing trill.
Habitat Scrub and thickets.
Range Western US and Canada as far north as Alaskan panhandle.
Movements Summer visitor.

Wilson's Warbler

Wilsonia pusilla 4½in/12cm

Identification Male is greenish above and yellow below with neat black crown patch; this feature is lacking in the female which can easily be confused with other yellow warblers that lack wing-bars. Female and immatures both similar to larger Hooded Warbler, but lack white in the tail.
Voice Long series of *chip* notes on a descending scale.
Habitat Ground cover in dense, damp woodland.
Range Boreal Canada and southwards through the Rockies.
Movements Summer visitor.

Red-faced Warbler

Cardellina rubrifrons 5½–6in/14–15cm

Identification Gray upperparts, white belly, with distinctive head pattern of red and black. Immature is less boldly marked with a pink flush on the 'face'.
Voice Thin *weet* notes.
Habitat Mountain forests, usually mixed.
Range South-western states.
Movements Summer visitor.

American Redstart

Setophaga ruticilla 5–5½in/13–14cm

Identification
Male is black with white belly and distinctive bands of orange-red at bend of wing, across the flight feathers, and at the base of the tail. Female is olive-green with patches of yellow where the male is red. Young male resembles female with yellow rather than red patches, but is darker and with a hint of orange at the bend of the wing.
Voice High notes ending in downslurred flourish.
Habitat Coverts and damp woods.
Range Most of North America except for north and south-western states from Texas to Oregon.
Movements Summer visitor; a few winter southern Florida.

Painted Redstart

Myioborus pictus 6in/15–16cm

Identification A black bird with crimson belly and white patches in wing and outer tail. Immature is slate-black, with white in wing and tail, but no crimson on belly.
Voice A pleasant warble.
Habitat Oak woods at altitude.
Range South-western states.
Movements Summer visitor.

House Sparrow

Passer domesticus 6–6½in/16–17cm

Identification Also called English Sparrow. Male has gray crown, white cheeks and black bib. Upperparts streaked black and chestnut, underparts dirty, gray-cream. Female dully colored with distinct creamy supercilium.
Voice *Chirrup*, repeated.
Habitat Cities, towns, suburbs, farmsteads.
Range Whole of inhabited North America; introduced from Europe.
Movements Resident.

Bobolink

Dolichonyx oryzivorus 7–8in/18–20cm

Identification Summer male is boldly marked in black with a white bar across the wing, white rump, and a creamy hood on the nape. At other times it resembles the female and immature which are streaked black and buff above, and buffy below. The striped head pattern; stubby, sparrow-like bill; and pointed tail-feathers are the best field marks.
Voice Loud *bob-o-link*.
Habitat Grasslands.
Range Right across northern US and southern Canada.
Movements Summer visitor; migrates south-eastwards to South America.

Eastern Meadowlark

Sturnella magna 9½–10in/24–26cm

Identification Medium-sized bird of open grasslands. In summer, yellow underparts with black 'V'-shaped breast band are clear feature. At other times streaked upperparts, striped crown, pointed bill and yellow-washed underparts identify. *See* Western Meadowlark.
Voice Whistling *see-you-see-yer*.
Habitat Grasslands.
Range Eastern US and south-eastern Canada, extends as far west as southern Arizona.
Movements Northern birds migrate, others resident.

Western Meadowlark

Sturnella neglecta 9½–10in/24–26cm

Identification Very similar to Eastern Meadowlark and overlaps range. This bird is grayer and less contrasting and has more yellow on 'face'.
Voice Bubbling notes.
Habitat Grasslands, generally drier than Eastern.
Range From the Great Lakes westwards.
Movements Northern and eastern birds migrate to winter along Gulf Coast westwards.

Yellow-headed Blackbird

Xanthocephalus xanthocephalus

9½–10in/24–26cm

Identification Male is black with buffy-yellow head and breast broken by black around eye and lores. Small white patch in wing and thick, pointed bill. Female similar, but with orange-yellow breast and brownish head; generally browner than male.
Voice Rasping buzz.
Habitat Marshes and farmland.
Range Westwards from Great Lakes through prairies and southwards to Arizona.
Movements Summer visitor; winters Mexican border; resident California.

Red-winged Blackbird

Agelaius phoeniceus 8½–9½in/22–24cm

Identification Male is all black with red, bordered yellow-buff, wing patches. Young male is scaled black with less pronounced wing patches. Female is boldly streaked black above and below with a hint of reddish on the wing. *See* Tricolored Blackbird. Forms huge flocks.
Voice *Kouk-la-ree.*
Habitat Marshes and fields.
Range Whole of sub-tundra North America.
Movements Canadian and northern US birds are summer visitors.

Tricolored Blackbird

Agelaius tricolor 8½–9½in/22–24cm

Identification Very similar to Red-winged Blackbird, but male has white border to red wing patch. Female very similar to that more widespread bird, but breast streaking is less clear cut and less contrasting. Forms huge flocks.
Voice *Ou-kee-kar,* harsher than Red-winged.
Habitat Marshes, damp fields.
Range Western California.
Movements Resident.

Rusty Blackbird

Euphagus carolinus 9–9½in/23–24cm

Identification Breeding male is all black with long, pointed bill and contrasting yellow eye. Female is slate gray with mottling on breast. Outside breeding season, all birds have rusty tips to feathers of body, wing coverts and tertials that gradually wear away to produce the summer plumage.
Voice High pitched *coo-a-lee.*
Habitat Damp woods and marshes.
Range Boreal Alaska and Canada.
Movements Summer visitor; winters over whole of eastern US except extreme north.

Brewer's Blackbird

Euphagus cyanocephalus 9–10in/23–25cm

Identification Male is black with purple gloss on head and green gloss on wings and body. The eye is yellow. Female is dull brown above and below, with dark eye. Some fall males are rusty on the body, but never so obviously so as Rusty Blackbird.
Voice Harsh, wheezy song.
Habitat Parks, suburbs, farmsteads, woods.
Range Western US and Canada extending eastwards to Great Lakes.
Movements Northern and eastern birds migrate to southern US in winter.

Great-tailed Grackle

Quiscalus mexicanus

(M)18–19in/46–48cm,
(F)15-15½in/38-40cm

Identification Male has purple gloss over body, with long, 'V'-shaped tail, the eye is yellow. Female is brown above, buffy on throat and breast, with shorter, wedge-shaped tail. *See* Boat-tailed Grackle, formerly regarded as conspecific.
Voice Squeaks and harsh calls.
Habitat Marshes and open scrubland.
Range South-western US from Texas to California.
Movements Some northern populations move southwards in winter.

Common Grackle

Quiscalus quiscula 12½–13½in/32–34cm

Identification Male is black with longish, 'V'-shaped tail. At close range a purple gloss on head and wings may be visible, though northern and western birds show a blue gloss on the head and a bronze gloss on breast and back. Female is brown with dark eye, but also has 'V'-shaped tail.
Voice Loud squeaks.
Habitat Suburbs, farms, fields.
Range Whole of North America, east of the Rockies.
Movements Northern and western birds are summer visitors.

Brown-headed Cowbird

Molothrus ater 7½–8in/19–20cm

Identification Distinguished from other blackbirds by stubby bill and small size. Male has chocolate head and black body with greenish gloss. Female is brown above and dirty buff below, with dark streaking. Forms large flocks.
Voice Harsh sqeaking.
Habitat Parks, suburbs, farms, woods.
Range Whole of sub-tundra North America.
Movements Northern and western birds largely summer visitors.

Bronzed Cowbird

Molothrus aeneus 8½–9in/22–23cm

Identification Thick, but longish, bill is characteristic in all plumages. Male has dark brown body with blue glossed wings and tail. A red eye may be distinguished at close range. Female varies from uniform black, to dark brown with slightly paler underparts. All birds have a ruff on hind neck that creates an unusual profile when raised.

Voice Harsh squeaking.
Habitat Fields, thickets.
Range South-western US.
Movements Winters southernmost Texas; otherwise only a summer visitor.

Scott's Oriole

Icterus parisorum 9–9½in/23–24cm

Identification Male has black head and breast, yellow body, and black wings and tail, the former with a white wing-bar. Female is streaked green above, with a double, white wing-bar; dull greenish below, with a black mottled bib. Could be confused with the smaller Orchard Oriole in some plumages.
Voice Pleasant warbling and whistling.
Habitat Yuccas, pinyons and other arid vegetation.
Range South-western US.
Movements Summer visitor.

Hooded Oriole

Icterus cucullatus 8–8½in/20–21cm

Identification Male is orange with black face and extended bib, black wings with double wing bar, and black tail. Female is greenish-yellow lacking any warm tones on breast, or white on belly. Bill is distinctly decurved.
Voice Whisting trills and gentle warbling.
Habitat Palms and other trees.
Range California and Mexican border states.
Movements Summer visitor.

Northern Oriole

Icterus galbula 8½–9in/22–23cm

Identification Formerly divided into Baltimore and Bullock's Orioles. Eastern male has black head, back and breast; black wings with a white bar; and black tail with rufous terminal margins. Body and rump are rich rufous. Western male (Bullock's) has rufous extending over 'face' and a bold, white wing patch. Female is brownish above and warm orange below, though western female is much paler, with warm wash only on breast.
Voice Fluty whistles.
Habitat Woods and suburbs.
Range Most of US and southern Canada.
Movements Summer visitor.

Western Tanager

Piranga ludoviciana 7–7½in/18–19cm

Identification Active, forest bird with thickish bill. Male's head is brilliant flame-red; underparts and rump, yellow; back, tail and wings black, the latter with double, yellow wing-bar. Female is brownish above and dull yellow below, marked by double wing-bar.
Voice Harsh whistling.
Habitat Conifers at altitude.
Range Most of the Rocky Mountain system.
Movements Summer visitor.

Summer Tanager

Piranga rubra 8–8½in/20–21cm

Identification Male is bright red with broad red margins to black wing feathers. Needs to be separated with care from Hepatic Tanager. Female is greenish-olive above with yellow underparts, variably washed with warm orange.
Voice Warbling whistles.
Habitat Oak-pine woods and cottonwoods.
Range Right across southern US.
Movements Summer visitor.

Hepatic Tanager

Piranga flava 8–8½in/20–21cm

Identification Male similar to male Summer Tanager, but with brownish ear coverts and dusky wash over back, wings and belly. A dull, scruffy version of the more widespread bird. Female similar to female Summer Tanager, but with gray ear coverts.
Voice Harsh whistling.
Habitat Conifers and oaks at altitude.
Range South-western US.
Movements Summer visitor.

Northern Cardinal

Cardinalis cardinalis 8½–9in/22–23cm

Identification Male is red with black 'face' and bib, conical pink bill, and sharply pointed red crest. Female is buffy-brown on head, underparts and back with red wings, tail and crest.
Voice Repeated whistled phrases.
Habitat Suburbs, woodland margins, marshy thickets.
Range Eastern US extending westwards along Mexican border.
Movements Resident.

Pyrrhuloxia

Cardinalis sinuatus 8½–9in/22–23cm

Identification Similar in shape to related Northern Cardinal. Male is dove-gray with red tail, primary edges, face, breast, and tip of crest. Female similar, but less red. Horn-colored bill is hooked, parrot-like.
Voice Thin whistles.
Habitat Arid scrub.
Range Mexican border states.
Movements Resident.

Black-headed Grosbeak

Pheucticus melanocephalus 8½in/21–22cm

Identification Male has black head, black back and tail, and black wings with double, white wing-bar and primary patch. The rich cinnamon underparts are diagnostic. Heavy, conical bill. Female similar to female Rose-breasted Grosbeak, but with much lighter, more diffuse, streaking on breast.
Voice Whistled phrases.
Habitat Woodland margins and clearings.
Range Western US into adjacent Canada.
Movements Summer visitor.

Evening Grosbeak

Hesperiphona vespertina 7½–8½in/19–21cm

Identification Thick-set finch with massive, pale conical bill. Male is a yellow bird, though the tail is black, and the wings boldly marked black and white. Forehead and supercilium, lower back and belly all yellow. Female is grayer.
Voice A House Sparrow-like chirp.
Habitat Breeds in conifer forests; visits feeding stations for sunflower seeds in winter.
Range Breeds across southern Canada, extreme north-eastern US, and southwards through Rockies.
Movements Southwards throughout northern half of US.

Blue Grosbeak

Guiraca caerulea 6–7½in/15–19cm

Identification Chunky, large-billed finch that is dark blue with rusty wing patches in male. Only other 'blue' finch is smaller, paler and lacks rust. Female resembles female House Sparrow, but is warm brown rather than gray and has two rusty wingbars.
Voice Song is rich warble; calls *klink*.
Habitat Hedgerows, thickets, damp grasslands and sorghum fields; roadside wires.
Range Summer visitor northwards across southern half of US, though absent from most of Rockies.
Movements Winters southwards to Central America.

Lazuli Bunting

Passerina amoena 5–5½in/13–14cm

Identification Similar in shape and behavior to Indigo Bunting, which it replaces in the west. Male is blue on head, neck and rump; breast and flanks warm rufous; belly white. Bold, white, double wing-bar. Female, warm brown. White wing-bars separate from female Indigo Bunting.
Voice Descending and rising warble with repeated phrases confined to opening notes.
Habitat Arid gullies with brush, poor pastures.
Range Summer visitor western US, though absent from southern arid Rockies.
Movements Winters Mexico.

Painted Bunting

Passerina ciris 5½in/14cm

Identification Male is highly colorful with purple head, yellow-green back, red rump and underparts. Bill conical and silver; eye with red ring. Female greenish above, yellowish-green below; pale eye-ring.
Voice Variable, mainly clear warbling.
Habitat Hedgerows, thickets.
Range Summer visitor to southern US as far north as Missouri.
Movements Winters Central American, though some stay on in Gulf states.

Purple Finch

Carpodacus purpureus 6in/15–16cm

Identification Male is a rosy-pink on head, back and underparts, with pinkish margins to the wing feathers. Female is streaked brown on buff above and below creating a highly contrasting, striped impression. In particular, the pale supercilium is more prominent than in related species.
Voice Pleasant warble.
Habitat Conifer and mixed woodland.
Range Boreal Canada extending southwards through Rockies and the Great Lakes area to north-eastern US.
Movements Boreal zone birds move southwards to winter throughout eastern US.

Cassin's Finch

Carpodacus cassinii 6–6½in/16–17cm

Identification Similar to Purple Finch with wash of pink over adult male. Differs in having brown nape; contrasting black and buff streaked back; streaking on flanks and undertail coverts. Female is less contrastingly streaked than female Purple Finch with less prominent supercilium.
Voice Pleasant warbling.
Habitat Forests at altitude.
Range Rocky Mountain forests from southern British Columbia to the arid, forestless, south western US.
Movements Resident, but some movement to areas where it does not breed.

House Finch

Carpodacus mexicanus 6in/15-16cm

Identification: Male has red band extending from forehead over eye, and a red breast. Crown and upperparts are brown; belly buff, streaked brown. Bill is short and stubby. Female is brownish streaked dark brown above and below.
Voice: Warbling with some nasal notes.
Habitat: Dry ranchland, suburbs and hillsides to considerable altitude.
Range: Western US; introduced in east where spreading rapidly southwards.
Movements: Resident, but may winter in new areas prior to colonization.

Pine Grosbeak

Pinicola enucleator

9–10in/23–25cm

Identification Largest of the 'red' finches, with chunky shape accentuated by smallish head and bill. Male is red above and below, with black tail, and black wings marked by white, double wing-bar. Female lacks red and is warm orange-buff on head and nape, otherwise gray.
Voice Low warbling with nasal ending.
Habitat Conifer woods, also deciduous woods in winter.
Range Boreal Canada to north-eastern US and southwards through the Rockies.
Movements Northernmost birds move southwards on irregular irruptive pattern.

Rosy Finch

Leucosticte arctoa

6–6½in/16–17cm

Identification Formerly divided among three distinct species, now regarded as conspecific. Male has brown back and breast, pink rump and underparts, pink on the wing coverts and a gray nape below a black crest. Though varying from pale to dark forms, there is no difficulty in identifying the males as this species. Female is brown with pale, double wing-bar. Confiding.
Voice High-pitched chipping notes.
Habitat Tundra, taiga and mountains above tree line.
Range From Alaska southwards through the Rockies to northern New Mexico.
Movements Resident, but does wander eastwards in winter.

Hoary Redpoll

Carduelis hornemanni 5½–6in/14–15cm

Identification High arctic equivalent of Common Redpoll, which it closely resembles. In general, a washed-out version with pale, buff upperparts, white rump and whitish underparts. Pink wash on breast of male, paler and less obvious.
Voice Buzzing trills.
Habitat Tundra.
Range Northern Alaska and Canada.
Movements Resident, but regularly seen southwards in Canada.

Common Redpoll

Carduelis flammea 5in/13cm

Identification Neat, arboreal finch with pink breast in summer male. Both sexes have red on crown and black bib, throughout the year. Upperparts streaked brown and buff; underparts buffy with brown streaking on flanks. Bill tiny and horn colored.
Voice Buzzing, nasal calls and trilled song.
Habitat Conifers, birches, taiga.
Range Alaska and northern Canada.
Movements Taiga birds move southwards to winter.

Pine Siskin

Carduelis pinus 5in/13cm

Identification Streaked brown and black above, brown and white below. Black wings show double wing-bar and yellow flash on primaries that is particularly prominent in flight. Thin, pointed bill.
Voice Wheezy, husky twittering.
Habitat Conifer and mixed woodland.
Range Breeds across boreal Canada and northern US to Alaskan panhandle and southwards through Rockies.

American Goldfinch

Carduelis tristis 5in/13cm

Identification Breeding male is bright yellow with black crown, black tail, and black wings marked by white, double wing-bar. Female is green above, pale yellow below with white, double wing-bar. In winter, the male is brown above with yellow confined to the 'face' and throat, the female is similar, but grayer.

Voice Trilling warble.
Habitat Overgrown fields, regenerating woods.
Range Breeds through all but southern US, extending northwards across the Canadian border.
Movements: Northern birds move southwards in winter, when the species occurs in southern states.

Lesser Goldfinch

Carduelis psaltria 4½in/11cm

Identification Small finch with stubby black bill. Male has black cap extending, in eastern birds, over entire upperparts. In western birds, the back is green, contrasting with black wings and tail. Underparts are yellow. Wings show white wing-bar, tips to tertials and primary patch. Female is green above, yellow-buff to white below with similar white marking on black wing.
Voice Trilling warble.
Habitat Fields, farms, hedgerows.
Range Western US.
Movements Birds in mountains move out in winter.

Lawrence's Goldfinch

Carduelis lawrencei 4½in/12cm

Identification Small finch, with stubby pink bill. Male has black facial mask extending to form a bib. Breast and belly are yellow; hind crown and nape gray; wings black with bold, yellow bars and flash; tail black contrasting with yellow rump. In flight, tail shows white centers to feathers. Female lacks black mask, but shows yellow on breast, wings and rump.
Voice Jingling warble.
Habitat Dry slopes.
Range California.
Movements Largely resident, but winters southern Arizona.

Red Crossbill

Loxia curvirostra 6–6½in/16–17cm

Identification Male is red with brownish wings and tail. Large head and crossed mandibles. Female greenish-yellow. Size, as well as size of bill, varies considerably. In flight, short tail and thick neck creates a curiously chunky silhouette.
Voice Warbling; distinct *jip* in flight.
Habitat Coniferous forests.
Range Boreal Canada southwards through Rockies.
Movements Irruptive across much of US on irregular basis.

White-winged Crossbill

Loxia leucoptera 6½–7in/17–18cm

Identification Similar to Red Crossbill, but marked in both sexes by bold, white, double wing-bar. Note white tips to tertials and smaller head and bill.
Voice Warbles, *chet-chet* in flight.
Habitat Coniferous forests.
Range Boreal Alaska and Canada to northern Pacific US.
Movements Irregular, irruptive movements southwards over much of northern half of US.

Green-tailed Towhee

Piplio chlorurus 7–7½in/18–19cm

Identification A large, ground-dwelling sparrow, with long, rounded tail, typical of the towhees. This is a well-marked species with gray head topped by a rich chestnut half-cap. A bib and moustachial streak are white contrasting with gray underparts. The upperparts are green.
Voice Whistled song terminating with a trill.
Habitat Dry chaparral at altitude.
Range Rocky Mountains of US.
Movements Mainly summer visitor, winters along Mexican border.

Rufous-sided Towhee

Pipilo erythrophthalmus 8½–9in/22–23cm

Identification Most widespread towhee. Male is black on head, breast and upperparts with white panels in the wing and white tips to the long tail. Western birds are flecked white on wings and scapulars. Underparts are white with rufous, chestnut flanks. Female is brown above, white below with chestnut flanks; the western female has similar white flecking as the male.
Voice *Tow-whee.*
Habitat Scrub and thickets, woodland edges and clearings.
Range Breeds over most of US and adjacent Canada, though absent from most of Texas.
Movements Central birds are summer visitors; elsewhere resident; winters Texas.

Brown Towhee

Pipilo fuscus 8½–9in/22–23cm

Identification Brown above and creamy below with large, conical, silver and black bill. Best field marks are a creamy bib enclosed by a necklace of black spots, and rufous, undertail coverts.
Voice Trills and hard, sharp *chinks*.
Habitat Dry brush areas, chaparral, suburbs, usually at some altitude.
Range South-western and Pacific coasts.
Movements Resident.

Abert's Towhee

Pipilo aberti 9½–10in/24–25cm

Identification Brown above, creamy below marked by a black 'face' that extends from forehead to behind the eye.
Voice A rolling trill.
Habitat Woodland thickets, orchards.
Range South-eastern California and Arizona.
Movements Resident.

Savannah Sparrow

Passerculus sandwichensis 5½–6in/14–15cm

Identification A brown and buff streaked sparrow with shortish tail and some yellow on the 'face'. Highly variable coloration, but all birds have a prominent supercilium (often yellow); a bold, double moustachial streak; and pale coronal stripe. Otherwise they may be heavily streaked, as in California; plain backed and lightly streaked below, as in Colorado; or totally washed out, as in the formerly specific Ipswich Sparrow of Nova Scotia.
Voice A repeated *chip* followed by a trill.
Habitat Open ground.
Range From tundra to southern California, but absent from many southern states.
Movements Mainly summer visitor; winters southern and coastal states.

Grasshopper Sparrow

Ammodramus savannarum 5–5½in/13–14cm

Identification A short-tailed, large-headed sparrow of chunky appearance and proportionately large bill. Streaked above; plain buffy below with light flank-streaking only in some subspecies. Most have a clear coronal stripe.
Voice Double *chip* followed by a buzz.
Habitat Grassland.
Range Breeds over most of US and border Canada, though absent from large areas of the west.
Movements Summer visitor; winters Atlantic and Gulf Coast states and along Mexican border.

Baird's Sparrow

Ammodramus bairdii 5½–6in/14–15cm

Identification A well-marked, chunky sparrow with clear-cut pattern of head stripes. 'Face' is usually warm buff with coronal stripe, lateral stripe, broad supercilium, double moustachial streak, and white bib bordered below by neat rows of streaks that extend over the breast and continue along the flanks. This is a species that exhibits almost all the facial markings by which sparrows are identified. Upperparts are streaked buff and brown, with rich chestnut on the scapulars.
Voice Warble and trill.
Habitat Prairies.
Range Prairies either side of Canadian border; scarce and declining.
Movements Summer visitor; winters Arizona and adjacent Mexico.

Vesper Sparrow

Pooecetes gramineus

6–6½in/16–17cm

Identification Well-streaked sparrow with short, white-edged tail. Lacks prominent supercilium of many other sparrows, but has dark ear coverts and clear moustachial streak. Chestnut shoulder patch usually difficult to see.
Voice Pleasant trilling.
Habitat Grasslands, farmsteads.
Range Breeds over most of temperate North America, though absent from southern states.
Movements Summer visitor; winters southern states.

Lark Bunting

Calamospiza melanocorys 7–7½in/18–19cm

Identification Male in summer is black, with thick, chunky bill and broad white wing patches. Female is brown above and streaked below, with broad buff wing patch and buffy supercilium extending around ear coverts. Winter male resembles female, but with white supercilium and moustachial streak joining to enclose dark ear coverts. Some black on throat and upper breast.
Voice Whistling trills, often in flight.
Habitat Dry grassland.
Range Central US and adjacent Canadian prairies.
Movements Summer visitor; winters Texas and Mexican border.

Lark Sparrow

Chondestes grammacus 6½–7in/17–18cm

Identification Brown above, grayish below with distinctive head pattern and small black patch on breast. Crown and face shows pattern of stripes in chestnut black and white. In flight, white outer feathers contrast with black tail.
Voice Extended trills and buzzes.
Habitat Prairies and other open areas.
Range Most of US except eastern coastal states; also south-west Canada.
Movements Summer visitor; winters Florida, Gulf Coast and Mexican border states.

Black-throated Sparrow

Amphispiza bilineata 5½in/14cm

Identification Neat brown and white bird, marked by black bib extending to a point on the breast. Brown head shows contrasting white supercilium and moustachial streak. Immature has gray head with bold white supercilium. White in outer tail, small bill.
Voice Trilling.
Habitat Dry hillsides.
Range Rocky Mountains from Oregon southwards.
Movements Northern birds move southwards in winter.

Sage Sparrow

Amphispiza belli 6–6½in/16–17cm

Identification Large, ground-dwelling sparrow with gray head; brownish upperparts, white underparts with flank streaking and small, black breast spot. White supercilium and moustachial streak are most obvious in much darker Californian form. A great runner.
Voice Series of thin notes.
Habitat Dry, arid flats, sagebrush, chapparal.
Range Western US.
Movements Resident California; inland birds move southwards to winter.

Dark-eyed Junco

Junco hyemalis

6–6½in/16–17cm

Identification Former division into four distinct species indicates variability of plumage. Male has gray upperparts extending to breast, with paler or white belly. Head may be black; back may be brown; belly may be washed pinkish. Most have pale, conical bill, and dark eye. Female is brown above and white below. All have broad white margins to tail.
Voice Pleasant trill.
Habitat Woodlands in summer; catholic in winter.
Range From Alaska to Newfoundland southwards, through northern US extending south through Rockies and Appalachians.
Movements Northern birds move southwards to winter throughout US.

Rufous-crowned Sparrow

Aimophila ruficeps 6in/15–16cm

Identification A dusky, long-tailed sparrow with chestnut cap. Gray-brown upperparts; pale gray underparts; tail, long and pointed. Chestnut cap extends to nape; thin chestnut eye stripe; black moustachial stripe make identification straightforward, if well seen. Spends much time on ground.
Voice Jumble of chipping notes.
Habitat Rocky slopes.
Range South-western states.
Movements Mostly resident.

Cassin's Sparrow

Aimophila cassinii 6in/15–16cm

Identification Chunky sparrow with heavy bill and long, white-tipped tail. Streaked crown and back; plain buffy underparts lack streaking, with white bib. Self-effacing.
Voice Whistles and trills.
Habitat Dry grasslands.
Range South-western states.
Movements Resident along Mexican border; more northerly birds move southwards to winter.

American Tree Sparrow

Spizella arborea 6–6½in/16–17cm

Identification Attractive, delicately colored sparrow. Upperparts are streaked, rich chestnut with prominent white, double wing-bar. Underparts pale gray, extending to sides of head. Most obvious field marks are chestnut cap and chestnut smudge at side of breast. Thin line extends from behind eye; small black patch at center of breast.
Voice Thin warble.
Habitat Taiga with scattered trees; winters marshes and neglected fields.
Range Northern Canada and Alaska.
Movements Summer visitor; winters over most of US.

Chipping Sparrow

Spizella passerina 6in/15–16cm

Identification A darkish sparrow, marked in breeding season by chestnut crown, broad white supercilium and thin, black, eye stripe. Gray underparts extend to sides of head and nape to form a collar. Upperparts dark, with chestnut streaking and white, double wing-bar. In winter, much less obvious with paler chestnut cap and gray nape.
Voice Rapid, trilling, *chip-chip-chip*.
Habitat Suburbs, farmland.
Range Virtually the whole of vegetated North America.
Movements Largely a summer visitor, but resident in southern states.

Clay-colored Sparrow

Spizella pallida 5½–6in/14–15cm

Identification Neatly marked sparrow with unstreaked underparts. Head shows buffy coronal stripe; dark lateral streaking; broad, white supercilium; darkish ear coverts; and neat moustachial streak on white bib. Underparts are warm buffy.
Voice Buzzing.
Habitat Prairies, thickets.
Range Prairie Canada and adjacent US eastwards through Great Lakes region.
Movements Summer visitor; winters south-west Texas and beyond.

Brewer's Sparrow

Spizella breweri 5½–6in/14–15cm

Identification Similar to Clay-colored Sparrow, but much less contrasted. Streaked crown and upperparts, buffy underparts. Buffy supercilium, dark ear coverts and thin moustachial streak.
Voice Trilling.
Habitat Chapparal and sagebrush country.
Range Rocky Mountains of US with extension northwards into adjacent Canada.
Movements Summer visitor; winters Mexican border states.

Black-chinned Sparrow

Spizella atrogularis 6in/15–16cm

Identification Distinctive gray sparrow with chestnut, streaked back and wings. Male has black around base of bill extending to form prominent bib, lacking in female. Both sexes have pale, ivory bill. Could be mistaken for Dark-eyed Junco, but chestnut back is distinctive.
Voice Plaintive start to trill.
Habitat Chapparal and brushy hillsides.
Range California and border states.
Movements California birds are summer visitors.

Harris' Sparrow

Zonotrichia querula 7½–8½in/19–21cm

Identification Large, long-tailed, pink-billed sparrow. In summer, has black crown and bib contrasting with gray sides of head, marked with a black comma. In winter, sides of head are buffy. Upperparts neatly striped black and buff with bold, double wing-bar. Underparts white in summer, but with buffy flanks in winter.
Voice Extended whistles.
Habitat Taiga; in winter open scrub.
Range North-western Canadian arctic.
Movements Winters central US.

White-crowned Sparrow

Zonotrichia leucophrys 7–7½in/18–19cm

Identification Streaked buff and brown above; unstreaked grayish below extending to sides of head and nape. Distinctive crown pattern of black and white stripes; only White-throated Sparrow shows similar pattern in some area. Conical, pink bill.
Voice Whistles and trills.
Habitat Open areas, scrub, grassland.
Range Breeds across northern Canada and Alaska and southwards through the Rockies.
Movements Southern Rocky Mountain birds are resident; northern populations winter over much of US.

Golden-crowned Sparrow

Zonotrichia atricapilla 7–7½in/18–19cm

Identification Large, dark sparrow with yellow and black crown pattern. Upperparts striped black and brown with chestnut in the wings and a clear white, double wing-bar. Underparts buffy-brown with gray chin extending to sides of head. In winter, the head pattern is subdued.

Voice Rasped, three- or five-note series.

Habitat Meadows and waterside thickets at altitude.

Range Alaska along Pacific Coast of Canada.

Movements Summer visitor; Winters Pacific Coast of US.

White-throated Sparrow

Zonotrichia albicollis 6½–7in/17–18cm

Identification Large, ground-dwelling sparrow with typical hunched appearance. Bold pattern of head stripes similar to White-crowned Sparrow, but in some birds coronal stripe is gray and eyebrow a warm buff. In others, these may be white as in White-crowned, but with a yellow area at the front of the supercilium. White bib and rich chestnut upperparts are both useful features.

Voice Thin *dee-dee, diddla-diddla-diddla.*

Habitat Thickets in woodland and suburbs.

Range Breeds over much of temperate and boreal Canada into the north-eastern US.

Movements Summer visitor; winters through much of lowland US, especially in the east, but also in coastal California. Resident north-eastern US.

Fox Sparrow

Passerella iliaca 7–7½in/18–19cm

Identification Variable both in plumage and structure. Most have rusty rump and tail, many have gray crown and back, all have spotting or streaking on underparts.
Voice Whistling and buzzing.
Habitat Undergrowth in woodland.
Range Boreal Canada and Alaska southwards through Rockies.
Movements Summer visitor; winters Pacific Coast and across southern states.

Lincoln's Sparrow

Melospiza lincolnii 6in/15–16cm

Identification: Neatly streaked brown and black upperparts, with chestnut in the wing, contrast with whitish belly. Breast is warm buff, finely streaked black. Head pattern has gray coronal stripe, with chestnut and black lateral crown stripes and a broad, gray supercilium; dark ear coverts and thin moustachial streak. Somewhat secretive.
Voice Pleasant trilling.
Habitat Marshes and grasslands in summer; dense thickets in winter.
Range Boreal Alaska and Canada extending southward into the Great Lakes region and through the Rockies.
Movements Summer visitor; winters southern US; resident Pacific US.

Song Sparrow

Melospiza melodia 6–6½in/16–17cm

Identification Though highly variable, all Song Sparrows have a broad, gray supercilium; dark, moustachial streak; long, rounded tail, and spotting or streaking on the breast. Most show chestnut in the wings and the breast streaking, though variable, usually forms a solid spot on the breast.
Voice Varied clear notes followed by a trill.
Habitat Scrub and waterside thickets.
Range Most of North America, except southern US.
Movements Northern birds are summer visitors; winters southern US.

McCown's Longspur

Calcarius mccownii 6in/15cm

Identification Summer male has black cap, moustachial streak and crescent-shaped breast band. Otherwise rather gray. Female is buffy, with broad supercilium and hint of breast band. In winter, both sexes are buffy, the male with a remnant breast band. Thick bill, chestnut patch at bend of wing and black-tipped, white tail are standard in all plumages.
Voice Warbles in song flight.
Habitat Prairies.
Range Prairies either side of US-Canada border.
Movements Summer visitor; winters northern and western Texas and adjacent states.

Chestnut-collared Longspur

Calcarius ornatus 6in/15–16cm

Identification Unmistakable when breeding. Crown, margins to ear coverts and underparts all black; 'face' yellow; nape chestnut. In winter, buffy with black scaling on underparts; female buffy. Grayish-white tail, tipped black.
Voice Melodic warbling.
Habitat Prairies.
Range Prairies both sides of US-Canada border.
Movements Summer visitor; winters north and eastern Texas to southern New Mexico.

Lapland Longspur

Calcarius lapponicus 6–6½in/16–17cm

Identification Summer male has black head and breast broken by white line behind the eye that extends as margin to black throat and breast. Chestnut nape. Female duller, but with chestnut nape. In winter, loses much of summer plumage, or with chestnut nape in others. Always shows much chestnut in wings in winter.
Voice Warbling in flight.
Habitat High tundra; winters shores and stubbles.
Range Arctic Alaska and Canada.
Movements Winters across most of US, but not Rockies or southern states.

Smith's Longspur

Calcarius pictus 6–6½in/16–17cm

Identification Summer male is rich orange below, with orange nape and richly streaked back. Head is black, with broad white supercilium and cheek patch producing unique pattern. Female and winter male have striped crown, buffy supercilium and warm buff underparts, lightly streaked black. White outer tail feathers.
Voice Warbling ending in a flourish.
Habitat Tundra.
Range Extreme arctic Canada and southern Alaska.
Movements Summer visitor; winters in lower Mississippi area.

Snow Bunting

Plectrophenax nivalis 6½–7in/17–18cm

Identification In all plumages, shows white inner wing in flight. Summer male is white with black back, wings and central tail. In winter, both sexes have buff washed crowns, with warm buffy tones on sides of head and breast.
Voice Pleasant warble.
Habitat Tundra.
Range Northern Alaska and Canada.
Movements Summer visitor; winters from southern Alaska and Pacific Canada across whole of US and southern Canada.

Index

Auklet
  Cassin's 102
  Rhinoceros 102
Avocet, American 67

Bittern
  American 60
  Least 61
Blackbird
  Brewer's 195
  Red-winged 194
  Rusty 195
  Tricolored 194
  Yellow-headed 193
Bluebird
  Mountain 169
  Western 169
Bobolink 192
Bobwhite, Northern 55
Brant 20
Bufflehead 31
Bunting
  Lark 215
  Lazuli 203
  Painted 204
  Snow 226
Bushtit, Common 154

Canvasback 28
Cardinal, Northern 201
Catbird, Gray 161
Chat, Yellow-breasted 188
Chickadee
  Black-capped 150
  Boreal 151
  Chestnut-backed 152
  Mountain 151
Coot, American 66
Cormorant
  Brandt's 17
  Double-crested 18
  Pelagic 18
Cowbird
  Bronzed 197
  Brown-headed 197
Crane, Sandhill 62
Creeper, Brown 157
Crossbill
  Red 210
  White-winged 210
Crow, American 150
Cuckoo
  Black-billed 107
  Yellow-billed 107
Curlew, Long-billed 71

Dipper, North American 155
Dove
  Inca 106
  Mourning 105
  Rock 104
  Scaly-breasted Ground 106
  White-winged 105
Dowitcher
  Long-billed 78
  Short-billed 77
Duck
  Fulvous-Tree 27
  Harlequin 31
  Ring-necked 28
  Ruddy 35
  Wood 26
Dunlin 81

Eagle
  Bald 44
  Golden 44
Egret
  Cattle 58
  Common 57
  Snowy 58
Eider
  Common 32
  King 32

Falcon
  Aplomado 48
  Gyr 45
  Peregrine 46
  Prairie 46
Finch
  Cassin's 205
  House 205
  Purple 204
  Rosy 206
Flicker, Northern 124
Flycatcher
  Alder 137
  Ash-throated 134
  Dusky 139
  Gray 139
  Hammond's 138
  Least 138
  Olive-sided 141
  Scissor-tailed 132
  Vermilion 132
  Western 140
  Willow 137
  Yellow-billed 136
Fulmar, Northern 14

Gadwall 23
Gallinule, Common 65
Gannet, Northern 17
Gnatcatcher
  Black-tailed 170
  Blue-gray 170
Godwit
  Hudsonian 72
  Marbled 72
Goldeneye
  Barrow's 30
  Common 30
Goldfinch
  American 208
  Lawrence's 209

Lesser 209
Goose
Canada 20
Ross's 22
Snow 21
White-fronted 21
Goshawk, Northern 38
Grackle
Common 196
Great-tailed 196
Grebe
Eared 12
Horned 12
Least 13
Pied-billed 13
Red-necked 11
Western 11
Grosbeak
Black-headed 202
Blue 203
Evening 202
Pine 206
Grouse
Blue 49
Ruffed 50
Sage 51
Sharp-tailed 50
Spruce 49
Guillemot, Pigeon 100
Gull
Bonaparte's 94
California 91
Franklin's 93
Glaucous 89
Glaucous-winged 89
Heermann's 92
Herring 90
Mew 92
Ring-billed 91
Sabine's 94
Western 90

Harrier, Northern 40
Hawk
Cooper's 39
Ferruginous 41
Harris' 43
Red-shouldered 42
Red-tailed 41
Rough-legged 40
Sharp-shinned 39
Swainson's 42
Zone-tailed 43
Heron
Black-crowned Night 60
Great Blue 59
Green 59
Hummingbird
Allen's 123
Anna's 121
Black-chinned 122
Broad-tailed 120
Calliope 121
Costa's 122
Rufous 123

Ibis, White-faced Glossy 62

Jaeger
Long-tailed 88
Parasitic 87
Pomarine 87
Jay
Gray 147
Pinyon 146
Scrub 146
Steller's 145
Junco, Dark-eyed 217

Kestrel, American 47
Killdeer 70
Kingbird
Cassin's 134
Eastern 133
Western 133
Kingfisher, Belted 124
Kinglet
Golden-crowned 171
Ruby-crowned 171
Kite, White-tailed 38
Kittiwake, Black-legged 93
Knot, Red 81

Lark, Horned 141
Longspur
Chestnut-collared 225
Lapland 225
McCown's 224
Smith's 226
Loon
Arctic 10
Common 9
Red-throated 10
Yellow-billed 9

Magpie
Black-billed 147
Yellow-billed 148
Mallard 22
Martin, Purple 145
Meadowlark
Eastern 192
Western 193
Merganser
Common 35
Hooded 36
Red-breasted 36
Merlin 47
Mockingbird, Northern 161
Murre
Common 99
Thick-billed 100
Murrelet
Ancient 103
Marbled 103

Nighthawk
Common 117
Lesser 118
Nutcracker, Clark's 148
Nuthatch
Pygmy 156
Red-breasted 156
White-breasted 155

Oldsquaw 33

Oriole
Hooded 198
Northern 199
Scott's 198
Osprey 45
Owl
American Pygmy 115
Barn 110
Barred 111
Boreal 114
Burrowing 113
Elf 116
Flammulated 115
Great Gray 112
Great Horned 109
Hawk 113
Long-eared 109
Northern Saw-whet 114
Screech 108
Short-eared 110
Snowy 111
Spotted 112
Oystercatcher, American Black 66

Partridge
Chukar 56
Gray 57
Parula, Northern 182
Pelican
American White 16
Brown 16
Petrel *see* Storm-Petrel
Pewee, Western Wood 140
Phainopepla 174
Phalarope
Red 85
Red-necked 86
Wilson's 85
Pheasant, Common 56
Phoebe
Black 135
Eastern 135
Say's 136
Pigeon, Band-tailed 104
Pintail, Northern 23
Pipit
Buff-bellied 172
Sprague's 172
Plover
Black-bellied 69
Mountain 68
Pacific Golden 68
Semipalmated 70
Snowy 69
Poor-will 117
Ptarmigan
Rock 52
White-tailed 52
Willow 51
Puffin
Horned 101
Tufted 101
Pyrrhuloxia 201

Quail
California 53
Gambel's 54
Montezuma 55
Mountain 54
Scaled 53

Rail
Black 64
Clapper 65
Sora 63
Virginia 63
Yellow 64
Raven
Chihuahuan 149
Common 149
Redhead 27
Redpoll
Common 207
Hoary 207
Redstart
American 190
Painted 191
Roadrunner, Greater 108
Robin, American 165

Sanderling 82
Sandpiper
Baird's 83
Buff-breasted 73
Least 83
Pectoral 80
Rock 80
Semipalmated 84
Solitary 74
Spotted 74
Stilt 77
Upland 73
Western 84
White-rumped 82
Sapsucker
Williamson's 129
Yellow-bellied 129
Scaup
Greater 29
Lesser 29
Scoter
Common 33
Surf 34
White-winged 34
Shearwater
Manx 14
Sooty 15
Shoveler, Northern 24
Shrike
Loggerhead 175
Northern 174
Siskin, Pine 208
Skua, Great 88
Snipe, Common 86
Solitaire, Townsend's 166
Sparrow
American Tree 218
Baird's 214
Black-chinned 220
Black-throated 216
Brewer's 220
Cassin's 218
Chipping 219
Clay-colored 219

Fox 223
Golden-crowned 222
Grasshopper 213
Harris' 221
House 191
Lark 215
Lincoln's 223
Rufous-crowned 217
Sage 216
Savannah 213
Song 224
Vesper 214
White-crowned 221
White-throated 222
Starling 175
Stilt, Black-winged 67
Stork, American Wood 61
Storm-Petrel, Leach's 15
Surfbird 78
Swallow
American Rough-winged 144
Bank 144
Barn 142
Cliff 142
Tree 143
Violet-green 143
Swan
Trumpeter 19
Whistling 19
Swift
Black 118
Chimney 119
Vaux's 119
White-throated 120

Tanager
Hepatic 200
Summer 200
Western 199
Tattler, Wandering 75
Teal
Blue-winged 25
Cinnamon 25
Green-winged 26
Tern
Arctic 95
Black 99
Caspian 98
Common 96
Elegant 97
Forster's 96
Gull-billed 97
Least 95
Royal 98
Thrasher
Bendire's 163
Brown 162
California 164
Crissal 165
Curve-billed 163
Le Conte's 164
Sage 162
Thrush
Gray-cheeked 168
Hermit 167
Swainson's 167
Varied 166
Titmouse
Bridled 153
Plain 152
Towhee
Abert's 212
Brown 212
Green-tailed 211
Rufous-sided 211
Turkey, Common 48
Turnstone
Black 79
Ruddy 79

Veery 168
Verdin 153
Vireo
Bell's 177
Gray 176
Hutton's 177
Red-eyed 178
Solitary 176
Warbling 178
Vulture
American Black 37
Turkey 37

Warbler
Black-and-white 179
Black-throated Gray 186
Black-throated Green 185
Blackpoll 187
Cape May 183
Grace's 186
Hermit 185
Lucy's 181
MacGillivray's 189
Magnolia 183
Nashville 180
Orange-crowned 180
Red-faced 190
Tennessee 179
Townsend's 184
Virginia's 181
Wilson's 189
Yellow 182
Yellow-rumped 184
Waterthrush, Northern 187
Waxwing
Bohemian 173
Cedar 173
Whimbrel 71
Whip-poor-will 116
Wigeon, American 24
Willet 75
Woodpecker
Acorn 127
Black-backed Three-toed 131
Downy 130
Gila 125
Hairy 130
Ladder-backed 126
Lewis' 128
Northern Three-toed 131
Nuttall's 126
Pileated 125
Red-headed 127

White-headed 128
Wren
Bewick's 158
Cactus 159
Canyon 160
House 157
Marsh 160
Rock 159
Winter 158
Wrentit 154
Yellowlegs
Greater 76
Lesser 76
Yellowthroat, Common 188

Notes